Money Matters

Money Matters

ANGELA DE SOUZA

Are you tired of trying to get through each month, living only to make ends meet? Have you read all the books that promise *'seven steps to financial freedom'* but lead you nowhere? Or are you someone who has plenty of money but can't find any satisfaction in life?

Money Matters has powerful, yet easy to understand principles that will radically revolutionise your view of money. Best of all you don't need a huge bank balance as a starting point, no matter what your current financial situation, whether rich, poor or anywhere in between, these principles will challenge you to the core resulting in financial freedom and a life of contentment GUARANTEED.

Series

Contents

Sources:
I wrote this book so long ago that I may have used or quoted another author or speaker. Where I can I have tried to give due credit. However, in some cases I have lost track of who the source is. For the unconscious use of any such material, I ask forgiveness.

Introduction

Today I read about four hundred young girls that were rescued from the sex trade. What shocked me most were their ages - age two to age fifteen! Immediately after reading this I went into my two year old daughter's bedroom and watched her sleep peacefully. It was impossible to imagine her not being tucked up safely in her bed sleeping as peacefully as she was. I could not imagine what sort of person would want to have her for their sexual pleasure! Turning a blind eye to this information and all sorts of other awful stories from around the globe was no longer justifiable. Saying that there was nothing that I can do about it at that point in time no longer worked as a reasonable excuse as I knew 'one day' would never come.

Today is that day. Today is *one* day. Today is that day that I stop justifying my passivity and start making a plan to do something about it. I will be plagued by the thought of this two year old in the sex trade forever if I don't do something about it right now. There is always something that can be done, no matter how small the contribution, it can make a difference, especially if everybody did something small together.

This book is not about the sex trade or world poverty, this book is about why money matters! It was a generous donation that set up the organisation that was able to rescue these four hundred girls from the sex trade. Without money that little two year old would still be out there having who knows what done to her! Bottom line – all the good intentions in the world **can't** rescue people who are suffering – IT TAKES MONEY!

I hope that by reading this book you too will see what I saw today. You will see that we have a responsibility to get our finances in order, to generate money and to get busy either financially supporting organisations that are making a difference in the world or actually getting our hands dirty and getting involved in the physical world.

God never made money, man did. The Bible is full of direction for us in the proper use of money, how we should rule it and not have it rule us. I have failed to find any verses in the Bible yet, that shows abundant life and money together, or happiness and money together. I really believe that God wants us to live an abundant life whether we have loads of money or very little money. My motivation for wanting Christians to prosper financially is because there is so much that we can do if we have money. Sadly, the problem today, is that **money has most Christians**. They are in bondage, in debt and under materialism without even realising it.

> *There is so much that we can do if we have money. Sadly, the problem today, is that money has most Christians.*

My conviction is so strong that God never intended for money to rule us the way it does. If we have money, it rules us – how do we use it wisely? If we don't have money, it rules us – how do we get it? Even those who don't lust after money seem to be ruled by it – how do we live without it and still be happy? The point is, no matter how good or bad we are at having this idol in or out of our life, we still seem to be so focused on it. My challenge to those of you who want to read this book is; read this book, get God's perspective, and get out of debt and then move on and don't look back. No matter where you find yourself at the end of this book, let one decision remain. I will no longer let money be a focus in my life anymore! Lord, renew my mind, create a new heart within me and let me be free.

Take your time and read these words slowly and allow God to place His heart in yours to gain wisdom and understanding about the realm that God intended us to live in the first place - **in Him we live and move and have our being.**

Chapter 1
The Lie

The Lie

Figs Leaves vs. Tunics of Skin

"Some people are always grumbling because roses have thorns; I am thankful that thorns have roses."

- **Alphonse Karr**

This chapter is not for the faint hearted. If you are not willing to be completely challenged in the way you handle your money, in the way you think about money and in the way you spend your money, it would be best not to read this chapter and skip ahead to the next one. In the next few pages we are going to expose the lie that we believe and come into the freedom of truth - the truth that Jesus spoke about when He said, *"And you shall know the truth, and the truth shall make you free."*[1]

Most people live under the illusion that a little bit more money will make them happier. If they had just a tiny bit more they would be OK. Other people think a lot more money will make them happier but few people think that less money will bring them the happiness they desire. I've jotted down a quote from the TV Guide[2]. This reporter was commenting on his findings with regards to celebrities and their great wealth:

> "I don't see any real correlation between wealth and happiness with these celebrities," says Mr X. "The money does not seem to bring them fulfilment or happiness, and I don't think it brings peace of mind."

Mankind is "programmed" to live according to a certain system - a system that has been taught to us by our parents. They were probably taught the very same thing by their parents and grandparents. The system is modelled and very heavily promoted by the media. The

I don't see any real correlation between wealth and happiness with these celebrities

system is also promoted by our peers. It is a system that is perfectly normal and accepted by society and by every culture, tribe and tongue. It is accepted as the normal way of life for many of us and this is the only way we know how to live.

Ignorance Is No Excuse

The problem with this system is that most of what we know and believe is a lie. Explore this lie with me and then let us explore the truth. Hosea, an Old Testament prophet, gave us a warning from God saying; *"My people are destroyed for lack of knowledge. Because you have rejected knowledge, I will also reject you from being priests for Me; Because you have forgotten the law of your God, I also will forget your children."*[3]

God gave a stern warning that ignorance is no excuse, and continuing in ignorance will result in the absence of God's blessing on our children. Parents are still living this way, not bothering to learn about the correct way to manage money, leaving their children clueless, lost and alone in this area. The Bible is full of knowledge as far as finances are concerned and the pursuit of knowledge and understanding should be high on our priority list. We should hunger and thirst for more knowledge[4] because what you don't know **can hurt you**. I hope that the following facts will not outrage you, but give you the necessary knowledge to be set free.

An alternative to believing the lie is to view money in the correct way. This path many people choose to ignore – remaining ignorant *by choice*. This way is through the narrow gate, the way that is considered by most as radical, even referred to by some as completely stupid – but this way is the truth.

Truth can often be a hard pill to swallow, especially if it affects our wallet but the truth is guaranteed to set you free. So with that in mind and without further ado, let's get to the point and start exposing the lie.

As we go we will compare the lie to the truth, so that you can see how absolutely pathetic the lie really is. It all started way back in the beginning, in Genesis 3:6 when, *"the woman saw that the tree was good for food, that it was pleasant to the eyes, and a tree desirable to make one wise, she took of its fruit and ate. She also gave to her husband with her, and he ate it."*

It all started with the woman wanting what she saw. How many of us get into a financial mess because we like what we see and have to have it? We whip out the plastic and get whatever we want with thirty days credit free interest. And then just to make ourselves feel less guilty we pop something on the card for our husband too! Sound familiar?

Perhaps you are like me and hate debt. Perhaps you don't relate to this illustration. I am sure there is something that tempts you, that if given the chance, you will take a bite of its fruit. It's worth having a think about it. Take a moment to consider what you would be willing to put on a credit card without hesitation.

What is Your Fruit?

What is your 'fruit' - the thing that you can't trust God for or are willing to go against Him in? It could be clothing or nice things for your home but it may be more subtle than that. Your child's medical expenses perhaps – do you trust debt more than God's ability to heal or provide? Repairs on your car or home could be an area that tempts you. What about food? Do you trust God to feed you and your family or do you take matters into your own hands no matter what it might mean?

It started in the Garden of Eden, right at the very beginning of time. The lie vs. the truth began soon after the world was created. A woman saw something, liked what she saw and without thinking about the consequences, she took it for herself. The result was destruction

> *A woman saw something, liked what she saw and without thinking about the consequences, she took it for herself.*

for the rest of her life and her descendants. Everyone became slaves to the things that they desired. Is it possible that we are still living as primitively as Adam and Eve in this regard? Have we not grown up past the 'seeing' part?

Many of us are slaves to what we see and desire. Before we even consider the consequences, we take it and 'eat' it. It tastes good so we share it with others. This 'fruit' can be many things but let's look at it in the context of money.

As much as we would like to blame the original sin on Satan, we can't. He only put the temptation in front of us. We make the decision to act on the temptation and we bear the consequences of that decision. Unfortunately, we pass our bad decisions onto our husbands and children, starting a chain reaction that leads us to being slaves of that very decision. The decision, if we avoided it, could have kept us in the Garden of Eden forever, God's desired place for us, the place of total freedom and fulfilment, the place of abundance and peace.

Are you following my reasoning here? Take the Garden of Eden story and apply it to the life that we lead at the moment. There still seem to be two systems running at this moment in time; it didn't end in the Garden of Eden. The first system is the lie and that remains '*I see it, I like it, I buy it!*' or possibly '*I see it, I need it, I have to have it because there is no way I can live without it!*' The second system is the truth, and the truth remains that *my*

God shall supply ALL your need according to His riches in glory by Christ Jesus[5].

According To His Riches

God made it very clear that He would supply all of our need by a distinct and exact measure, 'according to His riches'. When God proclaims this, He makes it clear that He is not tight-fisted when it comes to providing for His children. His riches cover all of creation, so there is absolutely nothing that you will ever need that He cannot make available!

In the Garden of Eden, even though Adam and Eve had grieved God's heart terribly by believing the lie that Satan told them, He still took care of them. He knew that clothes made out of fig leaves wouldn't last or be comfortable for that matter, so He made them *tunics out of skin[6]*. He took care of their basic needs even though they weren't ready to admit that the lie didn't produce the satisfaction that they thought it would. This is an awesome little piece of the Bible because it takes the simple fact that God made them tunics out of skin and speaks right into the core of hearts. It is such a simple thing that we could easily miss it. It is such a powerful act of God. God will always take care of our needs if we let him.

Perhaps Adam and Eve at first said no thank you to God when He offered them the tunic because they were embarrassed, and thought they could take care of themselves? I would like to think however, that they had simple childlike faith and were instantly repentant. I would like to believe that they weren't hung up on pride like many people are.

Some of us use the lie day in and day out to try and take care of ourselves and we wonder why we are never satisfied. If only we could have simple faith to accept that we have a loving heavenly Father who will make us tunics of skin – **even if we have messed up**. Moments of contentment are fleeting when we are totally independent, but they never last and cannot satisfy.

Take a look back on your life and see if you can name any moments or material items that have completely satisfied you. Of course you can't name any! It is a silly thing to say because we know that *things* don't satisfy. I believe that only God can truly satisfy us in all areas of our lives, the rest is only a fleeting 'feel good' moment that doesn't last. Only tunics out of skin could satisfy Adam and Eve's needs. The figs leaves would have fallen apart in minutes. God knew exactly what they needed even before they had any idea of their need themselves. They knew they were naked and needed to be covered. How they were going to achieve that was still a mystery to them.

He Knows Everything

Often, we are like Adam and Eve; we make clothes out of fig leaves because we are desperate for a solution. We try and fix things ourselves rather than turn to God and ask Him if He has a solution for us. He knows everything. He knows the consequences and the life span of the plans we make. He knows what will truly satisfy our need. He also knows what won't last. We need to have more faith in God's infinite wisdom than we have in our own ability to provide.

I have some really simple examples to share with you, but you could apply this principle to many areas of your life. Many years ago, when my daughters, Lorah-Kelly and Jordan, were very young, I was redecorating my bedroom. I painted the walls a lovely lilac colour and I wanted all the curtains, linen and accessories to be white. After completing the painting, I went to the shops and bought some of the white accessories that I desired. Deep down inside I wanted to buy all the bits and bobs at once but didn't have enough money. The money that I did spend was scraped together in the first place. As usual, my impatience got the better of me. I wanted the satisfaction of seeing the finished project right away. I didn't want to wait. I chose to ignore the little inner voice inside of me that advised me to wait a while.

When I got home, I finished fitting the accessories that I had purchased and felt very satisfied with the end result. All that was lacking were some new curtains to finish the room off, but that would have to wait until the next payday. This satisfaction was short lived as two days later my mom gave me the most beautiful white bedroom set. She knew nothing of my desire for the bedroom set and that I had already purchased one. I could have kicked myself! If only I had listened to that little inner voice and waited. I would have saved the money on what my mother had bought and had enough left over to buy curtains.

Waiting a couple more days would have given me all that I needed to complete my bedroom. I realized that I should always listen to that quiet little voice that knows everything and wants the best for me. Most of all, if in doubt, wait! Thankfully, this was a small financial loss, but the principle has stayed with me all these years. It has prevented me from having more severe financial losses in other areas.

Fig leaves are our own solution to provide for ourselves and can't sustain us for very long. Tunics made out of skin are the real deal, the real provision, made to last. So often I long to get out of my 'fig leaves' and step into the 'tunics out of skin'. I think that if we listened to God when we went shopping He would provide bargains, discounts, or even tell you what not to purchase because He knows that a few days down the line something better awaits you. Although I don't pray whenever I do the grocery shopping, I do know that He watches over me and provides for my every need, one way or another.

Tested In the Little Things

Do you find this idea complete nonsense or do you think that these little things matter? You see, I believe that we are tested in the little things, and if we prove faithful, He will trust us with greater things. God wants us to be trustworthy. He wants Godly people to be ready to handle the 'more' that He has in store for them. Big businesses, cities, even countries need Godly people managing them. How are we ever going to get anywhere near to that level of trust if we can't be trusted with wisdom and common sense in our every day financial management?

Perhaps the significance is not on us saving a few hundred pounds but the emphasis is on whether or not we trust Him in our everyday life with the little things.

Is it possible that we are wearing fig leaves and won't let God make us 'tunics out of skin'? It is obvious that we can't change the original sin, but we should at least try and move on from there? If you recognise that the lifestyle that you have been leading is not the way it should be, simply repent and allow God to make you 'tunics out of skin'.

What Is Your Apple?

He will lead the way to abundance if you allow Him to; all we have to do is take the first step. Step away from the 'apple' (the forbidden fruit that Adam and Eve had to face – their temptation) that Satan is showing you, turn around and take one step in the opposite direction. The apple could mean so many different things to different people, but the principle remains the same whether you are dealing with ten pounds or ten million pounds. All God asks of us is that we take the first step. He sternly says to us, "Put your hands in the air and step away from the fruit!"

From there you'll be amazed at how much He will do for you and how much He will teach you. Just learn to walk away from temptation. Adam and Eve's apple was quiet literally a fruit that they desired to eat. They wanted to satisfy their curiosity, their taste buds or perhaps it was their desire for a snack. Unfortunately God put that simple fruit there for a reason. What they assumed to be harmless was the very thing that got them banished from the Garden of Eden.

Too often we assume that the little things have no significance in the big picture? We satisfy our curiosity, our appetites, our hunger, and assume that there are little or no consequences. Start changing the way you deal with the little things in your life and you may be pleasantly surprised at the outcome. Whether you are rich or poor start with something small and see what happens.

If you feel God is saying that you should give a beggar some bread, do it. Heaven probably won't break out into song and the passersby probably won't stop to applaud you, but you have been obedient to what may have been the Holy Spirit's nudging. Do you see that these small acts have already changed your focus and taken you a little further away from the apple? The apple encourages disobedience, but as children of God we need to walk in obedience.

You never know, God might give you a promotion at work because He knows that He can trust you to be obedient. He may call you to a whole year of obedience in the little things before He can trust you with something bigger. What can God trust you with?

The apple could be your taxes - are you giving to 'Caesar' what is due to him[7] or are you saving money in that area so that you can give more to the missions fund? Do you justify your actions because you are giving a portion of your *stolen* money to the needy?

I am not talking from a place of perfection here. In the past I have wanted to give to noble causes so I had *saved* in other areas. Unfortunately, if we are not careful, we could compromise our integrity and be completely blind to it. We are fooled into believing we are doing something good when actually it is just a trick of the enemy to hinder the blessing of God into our lives. God can't bless any form of sin. Our spending and giving has to be done with the utmost integrity. Get away from that nasty apple - it will kill you!

If the apple is not your taxes perhaps it is impulsive spending sprees or lavish holidays. Perhaps you pay little less than you should on you tithe. Perhaps it is the simple fact that God has spoken to you about something small, but you don't think it is of great significance and you ignore what He has asked you to do. Instead of being obedient, you have taken a bite of the forbidden apple. The first step is always the hardest and I guess that's why it takes faith. It will never be easy, but the rest of the path is so very rewarding.

Hidden Consequences

As I said previously, the media strongly supports the world's system. It hides the consequences and pushes the benefits of giving in to the temptation! Emotional music is played to lure you into their advert, cute toddlers and puppy dogs tug at your heart strings. All this effort and money is made just to get you to buy their product. Advertisers then offer you easy ways of obtaining it by paying it off monthly or perhaps no interest until next year. Even then if you still can't obtain it they still have other ways of helping you attain it. We are programmed in the lie, we have been brought up with it and we teach it to our children.

Think of this example for a moment. You've purchase an iPod docking system on credit; you take it home, set it up and give it a test run. It feels good to have it, to look at it and to listen to the music, doesn't it? Of course it does, otherwise you wouldn't have purchased it in the first place! Is this feeling of satisfaction real? Sure, you have acquired something that you really wanted and it plays the music that you enjoy listening to. But listen carefully, what is it really screaming at you? If you close your eyes and be honest with yourself, you will hear the chains clanging as they are placed on your body.

You are a slave to that docking system. You will hear your spirit screaming because there is an element of fear, there has to be because you owe the bank money now. It might be interest free credit, but how many other things need repayment on that same interest free credit system?

There is no guarantee that you can pay this each month. No matter how secure you think your job is, nothing is watertight, and there **is** an element of fear. You may even deny that now, but be honest with yourself.

No One Can Serve Two Masters

You are not innocent in the Garden of Eden anymore; there is an element of nakedness. You're vulnerable! *No one can serve two masters; for either he will hate the one and love the other, or else he will be loyal to the one and despise the other. You cannot serve God and mammon (material goods).*[8]

Mammon is designed to be our slave and God is to be our master. We can't have both as master. Part of not serving two masters is in verse 17- 21 of Matthew 12, *"Tell us, therefore, what do You think? Is it lawful to pay taxes to Caesar, or not?" But Jesus perceived their wickedness, and said, "Why do you test Me, you hypocrites? Show Me the tax money."*

So they brought Him a denarius. And He said to them, "Who's image and inscription is this?' They said to Him, "Caesar's." And He said to them, "Render therefore to Caesar the things that are Caesar's and to God the things that are God's"

This passage tells us that money belongs to man's system. We should be obedient to man's system and keep within the guidelines of that system. An example is to pay your taxes diligently and honestly. Pay your TV licence, even if you think it is unfair that so many people get away with it, pay all that's legally required of you. If paying these small things were the difference between being obedient vs. disobedient or honest vs. dishonest, I would say that paying them is really important. You cannot put a price tag on your integrity.

Greed is another thing we are warned to watch out for in Luke 12:15-21, *"Then He said to them, "Watch out! Be on your guard against all kinds of greed; a man's life does not consist in the abundance of his possessions."*

21

And He told them this parable: "The ground of a certain rich man produced a good crop. He thought to himself, 'what shall I do? I have no place to store my crops.'

Then he said, 'This is what I'll do. I will tear down my barns and build bigger ones, and then I will store up all my grain and my goods. And I'll say to myself, "You have plenty of good things laid up for many years. Take life easy; eat, drink and be merry."

But God said to him, 'You fool! This very night your life will be demanded from you. Then who will get what you have prepared for yourself?' This is how it will be with anyone who stores up things for himself but is not rich toward God."

The Good Life Has Nothing to Do With Wealth

Jesus says that the good life has nothing to do with being wealthy, so be on guard against greed. This is the exact opposite of what our society usually says. Advertisers spend billions of pounds to entice us to think that if we buy more of their products we will be happier, more fulfilled, and more comfortable.

How do you respond to the constant pressure to buy? The rich man in Jesus' story dies before he could begin to use what was stored in his big barns. Planning for retirement – preparing for life before death is wise. Neglecting life after death is disastrous. If you accumulate wealth only to enrich yourself, with no concern for helping others, you will enter eternity empty-handed.

Never say that I can't afford to invest. It's like saying that I can't afford to have money given to me for nothing. Think carefully, even the master in the Bible spoke of making his money work for him in Luke 19:11-27. The one who wrapped his money in a cloth had it all taken away from him and the ones who invested had much more added to them. We shouldn't be too scared to invest. The risk is that we will lose the little that we have and end up with nothing anyway.

> *If you accumulate wealth only to enrich yourself, with no concern for helping others, you will enter eternity empty-handed.*

The least that we should do, according to this verse, is to put it into the bank to get interest.

Each one of us has the ability to invest our money in some way. If you are really poor, you might want to take a small amount of money and put it in a fixed deposit bank account for a while. If you have a little more money, invest in stocks and bonds. Quite possibly you have a talent, take a small portion of your money and put it into your talent and then use the talent to grow your money.

My daughter, at six years old, realized that she could paint so she started to paint pictures and selling them to our friends and neighbours. This way she earned some pocket money. Later, she discovered the joy of taking a seed and watching it turning into plants. She planted her little seeds and grew plants to sell. I could go on forever at how industrious my daughter has been. The examples are very simple, childish examples but the principles behind them remain the same. The more money you have the more you can invest. Don't say that you're poor because you had no opportunities. If a six year old can do it, so can you!

Ice Cream Cones and Post-It-Notes

"A determined immigrant named Ernest Hamwi was trying his best to sell thin Persian waffles at the 1905 World's Fair. He worked sun up to sun down...he gave away free samples to everyone who walked past his waffle stand...but nothing seemed to work. No one wanted to buy his waffles.

To make matters worse, day after day thousands of hot, hungry fair goers would rush past Ernest's lonely waffle booth on their way to stand in line at the ice cream booth two doors down. Ernest would spend his long days watching the ice cream vendor rake in money hand over fist. Talk about adding insult to injury!

On one especially hot, crowded afternoon, Ernest's fortune took a sudden turn for the better. The ice cream was selling so fast that the vendor ran out of dishes. In desperation, he ran down to Ernest's waffle stand, begging for extra plates.

Ernest didn't have any plates. All he had were stacks and stacks of soft, sweet Persian waffles that he couldn't even give away. Suddenly, Ernest had an idea. Maybe he could roll one of his waffles up into a cone that would hold a scoop of ice cream. Sure enough, the cone worked like a charm - and that was the beginning of the world's love affair with the ice cream cone.

A 3M employee was looking for a way to keep his bookmark from falling out of his hymn book during church choir practice. He explained his problem during a brainstorming meeting at the office. A chemical engineer remembered a failed experiment with a new adhesive, and suggested applying it to the back of a notepad. That unlikely marriage between a notepad and a failed adhesive ended up becoming the Post-It-Note®, a product that produces billions of dollars in revenue for 3M each and every year!"

Failures Are Opportunities

Don't disregard your ideas and innovations, I'm not saying that you all have an 'ice-cream cone' idea; I'm just saying that God gave us talents and too often we don't pursue them because we think we are being silly. Don't you think Ernest may also have had that feeling? Maybe he did, but he still went for it. What would have happened if he didn't go for it and just said; "Sorry sir I don't have any plates"? Just think about it for a minute.

What about your failures? Do you just quit when it looks like you have failed, or do you ask God if it can be used? Give it a try, you might be very surprised.

"Oseola McCarthy has lived a tough life, that's for sure. At age eight she was forced to drop out of second grade to help her mother wash and iron the neighbours clothes. Seventy years later, Oseola was still working as a washerwoman. She charged $1.50 to $2.00 for a bundle – that's a week's worth of laundry for a family of four – until

the end of WWII. After the war she increased her price to $10 per bundle. Even in her best year, working 10 hours a day, six days a week, Oseola McCarthy never earned more than $9000.

Oseola was 40 years old when she was finally able to start saving money. She squirreled away pennies and nickels at first...then quarters...and eventually dollar bills. She put her savings in a local bank and never touched it. Over time, her savings added up, and the principle and interest on those savings kept building and building.

In the summer of 1995, Oseola McCarthy – the elementary school dropout donated $150000 to the University of Southern Mississippi.

How is it that an average woman with below average education and income can accumulate a small fortune? In Oseola's own words, "The secret to building a fortune is compounding interest."

Oseola's circumstances were extreme and in wartime, how much more could be done in our present circumstances. There are so many opportunities for us in this day and age that we shouldn't let them pass us by. We complain too quickly and in the midst of our complaining, amazing opportunities could pass us by."

Change the Way You Do Things

In August of 2000 I found myself in the terrible position of being unemployed. That wasn't so bad; the terrible part was that my husband, Mo (I changed his name for privacy), was unemployed at the same time too. My first marriage was a roller coaster ride of unemployment and employment – for ten years we were on this dreadful ride. We had lost everything we had financially and materially and were in the process or rebuilding our life. Both our children were at school and all the normal expenses that applied to life applied to us, of course. On top of all that we also had a car and a washing machine that we had purchased on credit that we were still paying off.

With all this piling up on me I decided enough was enough! I had had enough of battling financially all the time and I desperately needed to see something to change. Pure frustrations led me to open a savings account for each of my children and a savings account for us. In our three savings accounts we committed to R20 (South African Rands) per month minimum saving each. I was determined, we didn't really have the R60 to spare each month but I made it happen no matter what it took.

At the same time I invested in some Unit Trusts. Again it was a small investment – but it was an investment none the less. Finding the money was a challenge, but I have never regretted it. Ever since my initial deposit of R20 I had felt that I was one step farther than I had ever been before in my life, not because we had loads of money suddenly but because finally I was in control of our money and our money wasn't in control of me.

Many times, we simply have to take control and change the way we do things. At that time for me it was changing the fact that we were always in debt and never had savings. How did I change that? By first paying off the debt then saving! Even though it was painful it was worth it. This simple change turned around one of the many negative patterns in our life.

Is God Waiting For You To Move?

Praying and waiting for God to move in your finances may not work. God may be waiting for you to make the first move. When you take that first step the whole of heaven kicks in gear and goes into operation. Just like when Peter took the first brave step, got out of the boat and into the water. Suddenly he found himself doing things that he never realised he could do. If he had never taken that first step, he would never have known that he could walk on water.

Two kingdoms with two different economic functions are operating in this world. Man's system and God's system. Man's system works on buying and selling, Gods system works on giving and receiving. The world focuses its system on percentage increase; God's system is based on multiplication - a different set of principles entirely. The laws of increase are operated by the measure that you use. The laws of harvest use seed power and this is God's chosen method.

Seeds Are Determined To Grow

Seeds are determined to grow, have you ever noticed a seed growing through a tar road - you can't stop a seed from growing. They grow in rocky surfaces, hard ground and out of the side of your wall. Seeds are designed to grow. Even if the world's finances are crashing, seedtime and harvest will keep going. God promised that no matter what happens, seedtime and harvest would *never* cease.

The lie that would keep you away from this investment is the lie that once you have given to God you will never see that money again. That is a lie! The truth is that if you invest in God's kingdom, your seed will grow and your returns will be so great that you won't have room enough to contain it!

Chapter 2

Investment
Opportunities

Investment
Opportunities

Seeds must grow

Investment #1: Tithe

Give 10% of your income to your local church

"Bring all the tithes into the storehouse, that there may be food in My house, And try me in this, says the Lord of hosts, If I will not open for you the windows of heaven And pour out for you such a blessing that there will not be room enough to receive it. And I will rebuke the devourer for your sakes, so that he will not destroy the fruit of your ground, Nor shall the vine fail to bear fruit for you in the field, says the Lord of hosts."

- **Malachi 3:10-11**

Your Tithe Guarantee

What does this guarantee? I can say that this is a guarantee because it says, "And try me in this" In fact, it's more than a guarantee, it's a challenge – a DARE. When I was a young Christian, I read about tithing and decided to try it out. In fact I was so 'green' that for months I referred to it as my 'tith'. I had not heard about tithing in church but had only read about it in my Bible and didn't realise how to pronounce the word! From the day I met Jesus I took the Bible literally and was so excited to do everything that it said I should do, and that included giving my 'tith'!

I had very little money in those days but that didn't deter me. I was set on the fact that tithing was the right thing to do. Ten percent was my starting point in obedience to the Bible. It wasn't long before I increased my giving to fifteen percent then twenty percent. I just couldn't give enough. Of course the tithe strictly speaking is ten percent because tithe literally means one tenth. I didn't know this at the time I just wanted to give and so increased my tithe to include an offering too. Being a new Christian is really special, God felt so close back then and it's a pity that most of us lose that simple faith as we get older and 'wiser'. I was earning R1500 at that time (I was in South Africa so it was in Rands). Not long after I had started tithing, a woman came up to me at church and handed me an envelope, simply saying that God had told her to give this to me.

When I got home my eyes nearly popped out of my head. The envelope contained R450; almost a third of my monthly earnings. Wow, God is faithful. I was completely bowled over by this awesome gift and continued to give, which resulted in continued miraculous provision. At one point I was giving one third of my salary to the church and I knew that God would take care of me no matter what!

Return #1: Absolute Protection
Open for you the windows of heaven
And pour out for you such a blessing
That there will not be room enough to receive it
What earthly institution can guarantee this sort of return – none that I have ever heard of? This verse

is a promise to keep your money from being 'wasted'. How many of us have car repairs that keep piling up, unexplained expenses that creep in out of the blue, perhaps lost money or huge bank charges.

There are all kinds of ways that the devourer comes to steal your money. Only once you know the blessing of having the devourer rebuked will you really see how much you save. Parking tickets, medical bills, accidents at school, car accidents or breakdowns, dental surgery, theft, money lost, etc, to name but a few are ways in which the devourer can cripple you.

> *Only once you know the blessing of having the devourer rebuked will you really see how much you save.*

I'm not saying that if you have any of the above Satan is robbing you; I am saying that if you are right with God in the area of your finances you will see very few of the above bills. I am always amazed at how my first car just kept going and going and going. I never had to spend a lot of money on parts or breakdowns, etc. That little car just kept going and going, even the tyres seemed to last longer than most.

There are so many things that I could mention and I can really see that the devourer has been rebuked many times in my life over the years. Don't only see the miraculous as God provision; see the day to day savings that He provides for you as part of His awesome provision for you.

Investment #2: Give

Any form of generosity in addition to your tithe is covered in this investment. This doesn't only apply to money but to any area of giving including giving your money. The guarantee is that whatever you give you will get back in abundance.

"Give, and it will be given to you: good measure, pressed down, shaken together, and running over will be put into your bosom. For with the same measure that you use, it will be measured back to you."

-   **Luke 6:38**

Return #2: Absolute Abundance

It will be given to you: good measure, pressed down, shaken together, and running over will be put into your bosom.

> "There is a universal law of divine reciprocity. You give; God gives in return. When you plant a seed, the ground yields a harvest. That is a reciprocal relationship. The ground can only give to you as you give to the ground. You put your money in the bank, and the bank returns interest. That is reciprocity.
>
> But many people want something for nothing when it comes to the things of God. They know that it does not work that way in the world system. Yet they always expect God to send them something when they have not invested in the kingdom of God.

> *Many people want something for nothing when it comes to the things of God.*

If you are not investing your time, talent, commitment, and your money, why do you want something? How can you get something when you have not planted any seed? How can you expect God to honour your desire when you have not honoured His command to give? Prosperity begins with investment."[B]

You Can't Out Give God

Giving in obedience to God has the greatest returns. Often it might seem like a huge sacrifice, but God sees your faith and won't let you down. He seldom provides in the way you expect, but He always knows what is best for you. When you need Him the most He will always be there. I remember about a year ago, I attended a woman's retreat and during the worship God put it on my heart to give R1000 into the offering for the guest speaker. At that time I didn't have one penny to spare. Even my conference fee was covered by a sponsor - there was no way that I could have paid for myself to attend let alone give the R1000 gift to a guest speaker.

God was clear and He confirmed to me that that was what He wanted me to trust Him for. What could I do? I simply said, "Yes Lord! I don't have the money but I will trust you for the money to give."

I stood up in front of the congregation and shared what God had said to me and challenged others to ask God what He would say to them concerning the offering. My deepest desire was for everyone to hear from God and not just put their pocket change in the offering basket. Continuing in my plea I mentioned to them that it may put us out of our comfort zones but it is always worth obeying God. I still can't believe that I said that, at the time I had never done any public speaking. In fact the speaking in public probably took more faith and courage than the faith I needed to trust God for the R1000.

It was the Sunday on the weekend conference when this all took place. The very next day I went about my daily business and wondered how God was going to provide. It wasn't worry at all but merely curiosity as there was absolutely nothing that I could have done at all. God had to provide, that was the one and only option and I knew He would I was just curious as to how He was going to do it.

As I drove past the cash machine I decided to check if God had put the money in the bank. (I didn't really expect anything to be there, I hoped that it was that simple but I knew that it was highly unlikely.) Well what happened next was completely unexpected! You guessed right, the money WAS in my bank account. There it was, R1400, sitting there on the cash machine screen, staring straight at me.

At first I didn't believe it, then I wanted to jump for joy, but I didn't think the people behind me would have been too impressed. I quietly withdrew the money then put R1000 directly into an envelope to pass onto the guest speaker.

I tithed R150 and took the remaining R250 to buy groceries for my family. (I had very little food at home at the time so this provision was much needed.)

"Now He who supplies seed to the sower and bread for food will also supply and increase your store of seed and will enlarge the harvest of your righteousness."

- **2 Corinthians 9:10**

Direct Deposits from Heaven

No, God did not make the deposit directly from heaven, although that would have been pretty amazing but there is no money in heaven, only streets of gold.   What happened was that some insurance money that was owed to me was paid out. I never ever expected it to be that much money but God will use anything to get money to us if we trust Him. Ever since that occasion I have had no problem saying yes Lord, even if I can't see how it will happen. I have had many miraculous experiences like this one since and God has always been faithful in providing seed for me to sow and bread for food.

Let's digress a little here, I have to tell you a really funny joke that I heard recently!

"There once was a rich man who was near death. He was very grieved because he had worked so hard for his money and he wanted to take it with him to heaven. So he began to pray that he might be able to take some of his wealth with him. An angel hears his plea and appears to him. "Sorry, but you can't take your wealth with you."

The man implores the angel to speak to God to see if He might bend the rules. The man continues to pray that his wealth could follow him.

The angel reappears and informs the man that God has decided to allow him to take one suitcase with him. Overjoyed, the man gathers his largest suitcase and fills it with pure gold bars and places it beside his bed.

Soon afterward the man dies and shows up at the Gates of Heaven to greet St. Peter. Seeing the suitcase St. Peter says, "Hold on, you can't bring that in here!"

But, the man explains to St. Peter that he has permission and asks him to verify his story with the Lord. Sure enough, St. Peter checks and comes back saying, "You're right. You are allowed one carry-on bag, but I'm supposed to check its contents before letting it through."

St. Peter opens the suitcase to inspect the worldly items that the man found too precious to leave behind and exclaims, "You brought paving slabs!"

I LOVE this joke; it really puts things into perspective doesn't it! We can get so caught up in what we perceive to be valuable and so obsessed with things that really don't matter at all. OK, let's get back to some serious stuff. Let us take a look at some more investment opportunities and focus on some things that really *do* matter while we are here on planet earth.

Investment #3: Give to the poor

"He who has pity on the poor lends to the Lord,

And He will pay back what he has given."

-   **Proverbs 19:17**

Returns #3: He will pay it back

Here is perhaps the most definite identification of God Himself with the plight of the poor. God makes Himself indebted to the one who gives to the poor. It's very clear, God will pay back to you what you give to the poor so don't be scared to give – you won't be out of pocket for doing so!

Who Is *Really* Poor?

Living in South Africa presented many opportunities to give to the poor and there were so many genuinely poor people struggling to make ends meet in life. England, however, is a different story. My husband, Eric, and I have learned that most people who claim to be poor are actually better off than we are. The government benefits system and social services are excellent in England which means that no one needs to live in lack. I once heard a 'poor' person complain that even though the government had given him a home and money for food, they did not give him a TV. He spent a good half an hour complaining about his situation and went asking what 'they' expected him to do alone in his flat without a TV.

Was he poor? Compared to what I have seen in South Africa, he is a very wealthy man. Not only does he have a roof over his head, food to eat, clothes to wear, heating, a toilet and running water but in order to get all these things he did not need to work.

Don't be fooled by people's sad story, some are sincere and they really are poor but most people in the UK have a different sort of lack that is not financial. The man who complained about not having a TV did not have any financial lack but he was desperately lonely. His need was relational and so any giving I might have done should have been in the area of friendship. Eric and I do give to the poor when there is a genuine need but we use wisdom and discernment to decide whether or not to give.

These are the investment opportunities that I've found in the Bible. Ask God to show you where you should be investing your money. We serve a creative God and you may be surprised at what He has to say.

Savings

Let's move on to saving - another truth that will set you free. I have found saving an incredibly liberating experience. I have moved from the lie of credit to the freedom of saving. Credit or payment plans is not evil but it is a vehicle that Satan uses to ensnare us. If managed wisely it could be a helpful tool but few people have the self control to use the system effectively.

My aim is to give you both sides of the story and leave it up to your discretion to figure out what system works best for you and what kind of lifestyle you are able to lead. Credit can be a useful tool and it can, if managed wisely, create a way for you to acquire a few items that you need. Unfortunately, 99% of us fall into the credit trap and learn the hard way that we don't have the self-control or discipline to handle this system.

I would encourage you to consider the alternatives first and hear my argument against credit before you decide whether or not this option is for you. I don't need to make a case for credit, just turn on the telly or read a magazine – it is all laid out quite nicely for you there. If you are in debt you don't need to run to the nearest church for deliverance, I am not for one moment saying that if you have got debt you have got a spirit of debt inside of you. You simply need to be wise in your choice of financial management.

The Devil's Tools

Two of Satan's main tools are money and sex. And these two areas are seldom mentioned in church. I really want to break open the area of money to you so that we can come into a new level of freedom. Debt tries to draw you into a 'now' position rather than a future position. It will try and get you to enjoy yourself or to buy something when you can't afford it, rather than waiting for when you can afford it.

Debt is bondage, an inability to meet an agreed financial obligation. If you bought a house on credit (a mortgage) please don't worry, it is very unusual for someone to be able to buy house cash these days and a mortgage is really necessary. We are not, however saying that it's ok to borrow money for absolutely anything that you please. But let us not limit God, if you have the faith then by all means; trust Him to be able to buy a house for cash.

Debt is a spirit and this evil spirit has a personality. Debt has two personality traits. First of all, it will get you into a position where you are unable to pay back what you owe. Secondly, it will encourage you to spend without logic, rational thinking and accountability. Debt is like a barrier between you and what is owed to you and what is due to come to you, because obviously if money came to you, you could get yourself out of debt.

Credit cards can become debt cards. Credit cards don't have to be a bad thing, if they are managed well, and used to work for you, not you work for it. I would also like to say here that unless you are absolutely sure that you are able to use your credit card wisely, don't go there. Frequent travellers use credit cards all the time because it makes their overseas travel much safer. For instances like these, credit cards are the wise option and if managed well can be a good thing.

The devil will do everything he can to keep us in bondage though, he may have limited power but he does not have authority unless we give it to him. He can only exercise his legal authority in our lives when we are disobedient to God's instruction. So if we give him no authority, then he can take none. The church of Jesus has all the power that they need; we just need to exercise our authority.

God is not a killjoy, His desire is not to punish us and ruin us by taking away all the things we like, and He wants us to prosper as the Psalmist says in Psalms, "Let them shout for joy and be glad, Who favour my righteous cause? And let them say continually, Let the Lord be magnified, Who has **pleasure in the prosperity of His servant?**"[10]

God takes pleasure in us prospering. Unfortunately debt can bring illnesses, anxiety, short temper, nervous trouble, fear, worry, and sleepless nights. In seventy percent of divorces, the root cause is money. Doctor's reckon that if people weren't in debt, their surgeries would be empty, because debt causes so much anxiety and worry and many illnesses begin with anxiety and worry.

There is a way to avoid all of this, don't get into debt. Beware of overdraft facilities, the high bank charges are a trap that catches too many people out.   "I'll write a cheque out now and on Monday I'll get money to put into the account!" The problem with that is what if you can't get the money you need on Monday and go into an unarranged overdraft?

The alternative to credit/debt is to save. Get the cash value of the desired item and write it down somewhere in your monthly budget then work out how much you can afford to put away each month, less any possible cash discounts and work towards acquiring it. I find this an extremely effective exercise because this buys you some time to think.

Often, you may realize that you don't really want it, but would rather have something else or you may realize that it isn't such a desperate need after all.

Sometimes, a friend or family member may even give you the item and then you have cash in the bank you can use towards something else. It does happen, give it a try and you'll be surprised by all the exciting things that can happen along the way. It is also possible that sale on the item would come up and you could save even more by buying it then. There are endless possibilities that you can take advantage of by saving.

Wait and See

I remember a time when I rearranged my house to make space for an office area for myself. I rearrange a lot of furniture to make the space but then realised that I needed a desk. I was tempted to go and purchase one right away (on credit of course) so that I could get on with it, but I knew that I shouldn't. So there was this wonderful study area with no desk. Well, my frustration turned to joy when a friend walked in and said that they had a huge desk that they didn't have space for in their new home and asked if I would like it. That was one of those joyous moments when I made the right choice and I was so happy that I waited a little while.

Another time I remember desperately wanting a fax machine for my business. Naturally the credit option was out, so again I waited. I prayed, asking God daily for a fax machine, I thought I desperately needed one or my business would look bad – everyone had a fax machine in those days. I spread the word amongst my friends and family that I was looking for a second hand fax machine and had no budget to buy one. Days went by; the days turned into months and still no fax machine. Why didn't God answer my simple prayer?

I can tell you why, because in that waiting time I hadn't needed to make one fax, all my correspondence was by email. I really didn't need a fax machine - I just thought I did. If I had gone out and bought one on credit I would have felt a real fool, the fax machine would have been unused.

Even if you don't have anything that you want to purchase at the moment - save anyway, you never know what emergency could arise. Can anyone predict when their washing machine will break down or when their fridge will decide to stop working? Saving also draws interest to you, and we all know that that's a good thing. It is a good habit to get into for so many more reasons than I can mention here, but as you save keep submitting to God. After all, He knows what is best for you.

At times He may have you save for a purpose that you never dreamed of. He might ask you to travel somewhere for Him or He may even ask you to give the money away and trust Him for the item that you were saving for. One never knows what God has up His sleeve. He works in mysterious ways that we could never understand, but we have to trust that He know what is best.

> *One never knows what God has up His sleeve. He works in mysterious ways that we could never understand.*

Consider all the things that you have just read and keep an eye out for the one who would lie to you and keep you from walking in the freedom of the truth. It is only when we know the truth that we can truly be set free from lies. Too many people are happy being blind though, they are comfortable and don't want to face the facts – the truth.

More Is Never Enough

"If I had a little bit more money I would be happy."

"If had had enough money to be comfortable I would be fine, just enough for the basics."

"If all my debt would just disappear I would be fine."

"If only I could win the lottery I would be alright."

"If my ex-husband would just pay his child support, I'd be fine."

The truth is that 'more' is never enough. As soon as we have more we'll start to believe that we need just a little bit more. The only way we can truly be content is if we make ourselves content with what we have. Let's try being satisfied with our daily bread. Work out for yourself how much is enough and live within that boundary otherwise you may end up in that trap that keeps you wanting more and never being satisfied.

"Two things I ask of you, O Lord; do not refuse me before I die; Keep falsehood and lies from me;

give me neither poverty nor riches, but give me my daily bread. Otherwise, I may have too much and disown you and say, 'Who is the Lord?' Or I may become poor and steal, and so dishonour the name of my God."

- **Proverbs 30:7-9**

Many of us say these things and really believe what we say; we truly believe that a little more money would do the trick for us. I was in the habit of thinking and saying things like this; I only realized that they were all lies when I got what I wanted. I got a little bit more money, and I wasn't any happier than before, then I got a little more money, but it still didn't satisfy.

I was so disappointed that I felt exactly the same deep down inside. I felt no more security, no more happiness, no more satisfied than I was before. I went through a season of having enough to be comfortable; in fact I had more than enough for the basics. Why was there still this huge void in my life? I'll tell you why, it's a lie! Money can't make you genuinely happy. Yes, all these things help, as the verse above says, (paraphrased) "don't let me be poor lest I steal and dishonour your name", but for some of us having more can be a stumbling block (paraphrased) "don't let me have too much in case I forget you".

When you are not depending on God for your daily bread, for your very survival, it's easy to forget to depend on Him at all. There are people that should be happier with less. They don't realize the dangers that they would be in if they had more and perhaps they are simply not ready for more. Other people have much and are just fine.

> *When you are not depending on God for your daily bread, for your very survival, it's easy to forget to depend on Him at all*

This scenario is summed up beautifully in Proverbs 30:7-9; *"O God, I beg two favours from you; let me have them before I die. First, help me never to tell a lie. Second, give me neither poverty nor riches! Give me just enough to satisfy my needs. For if I grow rich, I may deny you and say, "Who is the Lord?" And if I am too poor, I may steal and thus insult God's holy name."*

At the end of the day you have to trust God for His best, but trust Him completely with your life – be careful what you pray for as it may not turn out the way you might expect. Can I throw a real spanner in the works now? Some of you out there may have a lot of riches but are really miserable inside. God may challenge you to give most of it away and live with little.

I am not suggesting that you have to make yourself poor (this is not for everyone), but I am suggesting that you listen to God. He may be saying something radical to you and because it sounds so radical you have ignored it or doubted that it is God speaking. Even Jesus said in Mark 10:23, *"How hard it is for the rich to enter the Kingdom of God!"*

I have heard stories where God has spoken to high profile businessmen saying this very thing; "Give me ninety percent of your monthly income and live off of the ten percent that is left."

The business man obeyed God is happier now than he has ever been in his whole life. More money equals more responsibility and more responsibility equals more pressure!

"There is one who makes himself rich, yet has nothing; And one who makes himself poor, yet has great riches."

- **Proverbs 13: 7**

Maybe He would have you take a large sum of money and set up a young struggling couple up in business? Who knows what He would say to you, just listen and obey.

If you struggle to pay off your debt you are more likely to stay out of debt than if it suddenly disappears or if you win the lottery.

He only has your best interests at heart and even if it sounds totally off the wall to you, trust the Lord, I can testify to His goodness and He will never let you down. It might leave your hand but it will never leave your life.

Debt Doesn't Disappear

As far as having your debt disappear, that is also a lie. If you *struggle* to pay off your debt, you are more likely to *stay* out of debt than if it suddenly disappears or if you win the lottery. I have even heard of people that re-mortgage their home to pay off their credit cards but then continue buying on credit! What's the point in that, now they have more years to pay off their mortgage and still haven't learned how to manage their money wisely? The Bible is clear about money easily gained – it won't last!

"An inheritance quickly gained at the beginning will not be blessed at the end."

- **Proverbs 21:21**

I have always been very fascinated by the book of Ecclesiastes in the Bible, it tells a story of a very wealthy yet very unhappy man. Ecclesiastes tells of an old man who has lived his life, learned many lessons and in Ecclesiastes he shares his wisdom with us. He, like most of us, questions the meaning of life.

I have pulled out a few ideas of his that struck me as highly relevant in our quest for financial freedom. The meaning of life and financial freedom could quite possibly go hand in hand. I have used Ecclesiastes in the context of finances but this book covers so many more things that could bring freedom to our lives.

From Ecclesiastes Chapter 1:

"...Vanity of vanities, all is vanity..."

Solomon worked hard his whole life long; he 'toiled under the sun', noticed people come and people go and sums it all up as 'vanity of vanities' and 'grasping for the wind'. How often do we not feel like we are grasping for the wind, that we are never going to get there, that we will be exhausted before we 'make it'? I considered this in many areas of my life, both life in general and in my current financial situation. My conclusion was that if I wanted to stop chasing after the wind I should simply stop.

Stop Chasing

It hit me, that too often we are so busy chasing after the wind, and in the chasing we don't even recognise that we have the power to stop. Have you considered sticking with your old car? I decided to do that, instead of working even harder to purchase a newer model car, I would simply stick with what I had. Perhaps it would benefit from a full valet and a mechanical overhaul, but in doing so I could stop chasing after the wind. Buying a new car would only mean that after a few years I would want an even better one. When would the chasing ever end? I had to put a stop to it, no more chasing after the wind to keep up with the Joneses! My car, if proper care was taken, could last most of my life. My granddad's car did, but I do remember him being out every Saturday polishing it and taking good care of it.

My granddad was a fantastic example to me of how to take care of things and make them last. Looking back I have fond memories of my grandparents washing the dishes together. Once my grandmother had finished washing the 'light' bits she would call my granddad and he would scrub the pots and the stove. Their pots looked shiny and new until the day they died. My pots have been replaced several times already in my short life as I admit I didn't take good care of them. Today, when I do the dishes and see my pots, I am fondly reminded of my grandparents who lived free from chasing after the wind.

Perhaps war time poverty taught them a lesson or two that we could use today. Wise stewardship and taking care of the 'garden' of our life, is recording all the way from Genesis through to Revelations.

My car gets me from point A to point B and I intend to make my car last as long as possible. In that particular area, I am no longer running out of breath! If the time comes that I have ten thousand pounds to spare, and if God agrees that it can be used on a new car, then so be it, I will replace my car. For the time being, I am content with what I have, and that has taken one little pressure off of me.

Next in the chasing after the wind saga is my home comforts. Do I actually need a new sofa or do I just need a change because I am bored? I can't afford one right now, so I would have to really run hard after the wind to get the money together for that. Granted it would look a lot prettier than what I have now, but why should I tire myself out trying to acquire it? My current sofa could look very pretty with a throw and some cushions added to it leaving me to be content with what I already have.

If I did buy a new sofa the novelty would wear off far too quickly anyway and then all I would be left with is the financial burden to carry. It is one thing to save and replace something that truly needs replacing and to enjoy the satisfaction of the fruit of your hard work, but it is quite something else to live to continually buy new things for the sake of it.

Stay Focused

While writing this section I quickly nipped out in a friend's car to fetch the children from school. Wow, it drove beautifully, much better than my car... oops. I had decided to be content with my car and now, suddenly, I am unsatisfied with what I have again. Daily I have to choose to remain content. New temptations and dissatisfaction rise up all the time, but to be truly content is a daily choice and not a once off decision.

Driving my friend's car could have caused my imagination to run away with me. Schemes and plots could have been devised to acquire a better car, or I could simply have said to myself, "Not at the moment, I am content with what I have". Cutting off the thought before it evolves into a desire or lust is essential in the quest for contentment. It would be too easy to become miserable and distracted due to a sudden awareness of the faults in my car after driving one much better!

It is not always easy to take control of our fleshly desires. Often we will have to make daily decisions, sometimes even hard choices in the area of our finances. Paul sums it up beautifully in Philippians 4: 11-13 when he says; "I am not saying this because I am in need, for I have learned to be content whatever the circumstances. I know what it is to be in need, and I know what it is to have plenty. I have learned the **secret of being content** in any and every situation, whether well fed or hungry, whether living in plenty or in want. I can do everything through Him who gives me strength."

From Ecclesiastes Chapter 2:

Solomon, the writer of Ecclesiastes, mentions the pursuit of pleasure. He tried to satisfy himself with wine; he built houses and planted vineyards, gardens, etc. He basically gave himself every good thing that he could lay his eyes on. If you were to translate that to the year 2012, you could say that he bought himself expensive houses and cars, hired the best landscapers and employed many servants, went on frequent holidays and lived it up. In verse 10 he says, "Whatever my eyes desired I did not keep from them. I did not withhold my heart form any pleasure. For my heart rejoiced in all my labour, and this was my reward from all my labour."

Yet after all this pleasure, he is still found to be miserable. He calls it all vanity and grasping for the wind. This is how Solomon, a wealthy and prosperous man, felt after satisfying himself in every possible way. If he felt this way don't you think it's possible that we could too? We all need meaning in our work and in our life. How many of us are still stuck, thinking that collecting material possessions could bring us joy?

In The End You Die

I have tried this too and unfortunately I have to agree with Solomon that the pleasure of this lifestyle is fleeting. No true joy can come of it. In verse 18-19 of Ecclesiastes 2, we see that Solomon was distressed because he couldn't take all that he had worked for with him after he died. He had to leave it all to the man who would come after him. When we too are old and our days are numbered we will come to realise this. My hope is that you and I won't wait until the end of our days to wake up to this fact but that we will see it right now and take action according to this revelation. Life is short, very short. Decide for yourself what is truly valuable.

Have we put our focus on material possessions and money, or have we spent time raising our children so that leaving it all behind will be an honour for us. In verse 24, Solomon realised that it is a blessing from God simply to be able to eat, drink and have his soul enjoy the simple things in life – the basics. Finding satisfaction in the basic, simple things in life is where true contentment lies. I am placing a lot of emphasis on being content because if we truly want financial freedom we need to get to a place where we can be content and at peace.

Solomon was far from content. I am convinced that he wrote this book out of that place of deep dissatisfaction. Do you know the real reason that you are working so hard? Consider what you find worthwhile in your life – where are your time, energy and money being spent? Will you one day look back on your life and conclude that all the things you strived for were in fact 'chasing after the wind'?

> *Consider what you find worthwhile in your life – where are your time, energy and money being spent?*

69

In my life I found that there had to be a season of poverty before the season of riches. I shudder to think what I would have become if I had not gone through the struggles that I had been through. At the time I had no idea why God allowed these things, but looking back I can only say that each season was absolutely necessary. I thank God for it, I wouldn't want to do it again, but I do thank God for it today.

"Yet true godliness with contentment is itself great wealth. After all, we brought nothing with us when we came into the world, and we can't take anything with us when we leave it. So if we have enough food and clothing, let us be content.

But people who long to be rich fall into temptation and are trapped by many foolish and harmful desires that plunge them into ruin and destruction. For the love of money is the root of all kinds of evil. And some people, craving money, have wandered from the true faith and pierced themselves with many sorrows".

- **1 Timothy 6:6-10**

From Ecclesiastes Chapter 3:

"To everything there is a season, a time for every purpose under heaven."

Pursuing riches cannot bring joy; all it will do is lead you into all kinds of evil. Understanding times and seasons can however bring you peace. There is a time for everything under the sun, perhaps even a time for financial hardship and a time for plenty. The key is not to strive for either but to be content during either season.

We will take a look at wise stewardship, we will look into investments and savings and we will look into making our money work for us. All these things are good if they are on a foundation of contentment. Striving and struggling will do you no good and neither will forcing the wrong thing in the wrong time of your life. Ask God what your season is, ask Him why you are struggling financially, ask Him what He wants you to learn through it. Thank Him for your struggle and *count it all joy when you fall into various trials![11]*

Chapter 3

Giants

Giants

Conquering Goliath

"Goliath stood and shouted to the ranks of Israel, "Why don't you come out and line up for battle? Am I not a Philistine, and are you not the servants of Saul? Choose a man and have him come down to me. If he is able to fight and kill me, we will become your subjects; but if I overcome him and kill him, you will become our subjects and serve us. Then the Philistine said, "This day I defy the ranks of Israel! Give me a man and let us fight each other." On hearing this the Philistine's words, Saul and all the Israelites were dismayed and terrified."

- **1 Samuel 17:8-11**

An interesting parallel can be found between the story of Goliath and our finances. There are two possible giants attacking our finances - curses or debt. There is a battle going on with our finances, the giant is challenging us and we know that if we lose we will be its slave and have to serve it always. This threat often leaves us dismayed and terrified.

Curses

"This day I call heaven and earth as witness against you that I have set before you life and death, blessings and curses. Now choose life, so that you and your children may live."

- **Deuteronomy 30:19**

Moses gave Israel a choice, blessings or curses; he wanted them to choose life, to obey God and to experience His blessings. God will not force His will on anyone, even if the choice we make means death. He lets us decide whether we want to follow Him or not. The choice He puts before us is a life or death choice and God wants us to be fully aware of this and to choose life. A way, in which we can become a slave to the giant and death, is by having a curse over our life. Have you ever wondered why some people rocket to the top and others seem to struggle endlessly through the gravel of life? No matter how hard they try, the struggle seems endless and senseless at times. While the one struggles, the other squanders and wastes opportunities, yet gets ahead in all areas of his life. I had spent years being the one who struggles and have battled and wrestled and tried my best, but all with no fruit.

Freedom from Pressures

Then I discovered the work of Derek Prince who wrote the book, Blessing or Curse. You can choose. The caption on the cover is, "Freedom from Pressures you Thought You Had to Live With." I think that says it all! I highly recommend that you get hold of a copy of his book and study it; it helped me in my struggle tremendously.

A curse may not be apparent at first. Two people can start out on a very similar path in life; they can come from similar family backgrounds, have gone to the same junior schools, achieved similar grades and have had similar interests. Both may have had a dream of starting their own business in their particular field, but one may make it and the other may not have the same success.

The successful one seems to have breezed through life with all the details having fallen into place quite nicely, good deals seemed to have landed on his lap, his family life is just dandy, etc, whilst the other may have encountered obstacles every step of the way, he worked harder than the successful one but never seemed to land any major deals. His first and second marriage failed and his children don't want to have anything to do with him. Finally he too gives up and dies long before his time.

Coming Out From Under the Shadows

It may not have been clear to these two individuals why they were blessed or cursed, they simply lead life and dealt with whatever came their way. How many of us just accept what comes our way without any understanding of the spiritual realm. Neither of these men understood the forces at work in their lives. The source of light and shadow may have their source in previous generations. The Bible speaks plainly about these forces. In fact, it has a great deal to say about them. It calls them respectively blessings and curses.

Let us look closer for a moment, at the man under the shadows. He does all the right things: changes his job or place of residence; acquires further vocational skills; studies all the latest literature on positive thinking. Perhaps he even takes a course on how to release some mysterious potential within himself.

Yet success eludes him. His children are rebellious, his marriage under strain, accidents and illnesses routine. His cherished goals slip through his fingers like water through the fingers of a drowning man. He is *haunted* by a sense of inevitable failure, which he can perhaps postpone, but never overcome.

All his life has the sense of struggling against something he cannot identify – something amorphous and elusive. He feels at times as if he is wrestling with a shadow. No matter how hard he struggles, he cannot pinpoint the cause of his problem or get a grip on it. Often he feels like giving up.

"What's the use?" He exclaims.

"Nothing ever goes right for me! My father had the same problems. He was a failure too!"

The person under the shadows could just as well be a woman, of course. She has married young and started out with all sorts of plans for a successful marriage and a happy home. She finds herself, however, on an invisible teeter-totter- up one day and down the next. Physically, she goes from one problem to another always on the verge of health, but never quite achieving it.

Her son begins to abuse drugs and she herself has become an alcoholic. Like the man under the shadows, this woman, too, did all the right things. She studied books on nutrition and child psychology. In her pursuit of success, she goaded herself on from one effort to the next – each one demanding all the strength that she could muster.

Yet she watched other women, with less motivation or qualifications, achieve the goals she herself could never attain. As you look closer at the person under the shadows, perhaps you see something that reminds you of yourself. You feel as if you are looking at your own life – but somehow from a point outside yourself.

With a shock you begin to wonder if the cause of your problems could be the same: a curse going back to preceding generations.

Do you identify with this at all? It is quite possible that you are not a bad person, or a failure, or whatever else you have thought of yourself over and over again. It's a real possibility that there is a curse over your life and your wrestle has not been against flesh and blood, but against this curse. I am not saying that this is always the case, but it is a very strong possibility in many of our lives. It would be good to take a look at your grandparent's history, your parent's history and your past and see if you can find any patterns emerging.

In my family alone I could immediately identify several curses and that was without even doing any research into my background whatsoever. We have most of the girls on my father's side falling pregnant before they were married and before their twenties. (If only I had been aware of this when I was sixteen!) We have a history of divorce. We have a fair selection of sexual and other abuse, bad tempers and alcoholism. Financial insufficiency also seemed to be fairly dominant. This list came to mind immediately.

I am not going to go into my story in detail in order to protect my family, but I would encourage you to take a look at what you see in your family line and see if you can identify any possible curses. Take special note of anything that tends to repeat itself over and over again in your life or your parents and grandparents.

Often it could be such an accepted part of your family line that you are not even aware that there is a pattern in your life. I know of a man who simply has his father's attitude towards certain things. It is such a small thing, but he doesn't realize that his grandfather had the same attitude and this bad attitude affects a huge part of his life and a very huge part of his wife and children's life. This may not be a curse, but it is a pattern and it is a great reason why his finances are taking such a knock. He has been accepted that way, people close to him just say, "Well, that's just how he is!"

From Frustration to Breakthrough

I would like to suggest that you also be willing to take a look at yourself and your family history, and see if there are any small patterns that are in operation in your life that may be the root cause of your financial problems. It is also helpful to listen to what people close to you have to say. It is most often the people close to us that will tell the truth.

A curse is an annoyance. The effect of a curse is long term frustration. You will find that no matter how hard you work or whatever you do there will always be something that stops you from having breakthrough. You work just as hard as your colleague does but for some reason he gets the promotion and you remain in the same position for years. You reach out for your dreams and goals but they constantly elude you for no apparent reason.

You study and achieve the necessary qualifications to become the person you want to be but something always gets in your way. It's as if there is an invisible wall that you cannot break through no matter what you do!

Many people eventually give up and accept that they will never succeed in life. Others do silly things as a result of their frustration and end up damaging their chances of success.

After I dissected my family background, I took a look at my short life, and boy oh boy, I was not even twenty five and I could see patterns developing. My pastor very patiently walked with me through all the possibilities and prayed for deliverance in all the areas we identified. There was a great sense of freedom and accomplishment but I felt that although they were broken, they were still a threat to me. I was still tempted in the areas that I was delivered from. Freedom only came once I had developed a lifestyle of resisting and overcoming in those same areas. There are no instant results; it is a lifestyle that you need to develop a lifestyle of discipline and obedience to God.

I have given a few examples from my personal life, but there are so many more. The best way to identify whether or not you have a curse in your life is to read Deuteronomy 28. The first section deals with the blessings on obedience (verse 1-14) and the second section deals with the curses on disobedience (verse 15-68). Based on this section we can find the following indicators of a curse:

Constant lack of finances

Fertility issues or sexual health problems

Mental illness

Unexplained or repeated illness

Divorce and relationship failure

Untimely deaths

At this point, if you are still sceptical, I would like to encourage you to pray about the possibility of a curse in your life and ask God to show you things that you haven't seen, or haven't wanted to see. God will give you the truth and the truth will set you free. Also, it is a good thing to ask a close friend who you feel you can trust to walk with you in this process.

When I first started exploring these possibilities I had heard a sermon at church and suddenly realized that there was something that was not quite right in my life. I went straight to my good friend and shared with her what I had felt the problem could be. She prayed with me and advised me to share this with the pastor. I did and the whole process of restoration began. We walked through some really awful issues together and to me it was like I had someone to hold my hand. (To all the men out there who are reading this, don't be put off by my emotional state here. Women will tend to deal with things differently to men at times. Just bear with me.) I don't think that I could have gotten through this time without her and I am a new person because of it.

My point is, don't feel that you need to tackle these issues alone, they can be really difficult and a good friend to walk with you is not a bad thing. In times like these you can really cement a friendship leaving your friend to benefit as well as you. (Oops, off the subject again. I'll keep that for my next book.) One last point before we move on. If you suspect that there is a curse in your life, be willing to admit to your part in it and deal with it, with a heart of repentance.

Put Your Head Down and Charge

If you approach this whole exercise with a heart of stone and an attitude of blaming your ancestors, I feel you may hurt yourself and only do damage to those around you.

If you truly want financial freedom, put your head down and charge. Tackle the problem areas in your life persistently and systematically until you are sure that you have done all you can. The rest is up to God and our faith and obedience to Him. I would highly recommend that if you have identified the possibility of a curse in your life or if you would like to know more, see your local pastor for advice on how to deal with your situation. You will be treading on dangerous ground if you take the little bit of information that I have given, and try to deal with this alone. I have merely provided a few facts and testimony to help you recognize a possible root of your struggles, I have however only included a few facts to aid you in this process, this is not the full picture, there is so much more information on this subject so ask God for His guidance in this matter and trust Him to bring you to complete freedom in your finances.

Chapter 4

Debt

Debt

Debt is a curse!

So the best way to bridge the two parts is to start with the worst kind of debt – debt to God. This verse will be repeated in other chapters as it relates to many of our financial problems and I make no apologies for repeating myself in this regard. If learning to give your tithe and offerings is the only thing that you get out of this book, then I have achieved a good thing.

"Will a man rob God? Yet you have robbed me! But you say 'In what have we robbed you?' In tithes and offerings. You are cursed with a curse, for you have robbed Me, even this whole nation.

Bring all the tithes into the storehouse, that there may be food in My house. And try Me now in this. Says the Lord of hosts. If I will not open for you the windows of heaven and pour out for you such blessing that there will not be room enough to receive it. And I will rebuke the devourer for your sakes, so that He will not destroy the fruit of your ground, nor shall the vine fail to bear fruit for you in the field, Says the Lord of hosts."

- **Malachi 3:8-11**

God's People Are Robbing Him

Only 20% of the church is tithing! That means that 80% of God's people are robbing Him. Ouch, that must hurt Him a great deal. Why do we do this, what argument do we have against tithing? What is our excuse? I can list a few reasons why you should tithe.

It says in this Scripture that you are robbing God if you don't tithe. If you don't tithe, you are cursed with a curse, for you have robbed Him. God asks you to bring your tithe and offerings that there may be food in His house. If you tithe God will open for you the windows of heaven and pour out for you such blessing that there will not be room enough to receive it. If you tithe He will rebuke the devourer for your sakes, so that He will not destroy the fruit of your ground, nor shall the vine fail to bear fruit for you in the field, says the Lord of hosts.

Ok, you got me, I just about repeated the whole verse, but God has made it so clear there that I cannot make it any plainer for you to see. There are five awesome reasons to tithe and a dare to test Him. Now I don't know about you, but I don't fancy the idea of robbing God and I would certainly not willingly bring a curse upon myself.

Also, I would not turn down the awesome blessing that He has promised us in the last section of that verse. So people, if you want to get out of debt, I would suggest that you start with God because when the blessing comes from Him, (the one that you won't have room enough to store), you can pay off the rest of your debt. Also, I find with having the devourer rebuked, you have so much more spare cash to do the other things that you enjoy so much. So if only 20% of the church is tithing, doesn't it make you wonder why the church is not having financial victory? Church, get out of debt!

Once again, there is a link between a curse and debt. If you are in debt, look at your parent's past. Blessings can come down the family line, but so can curses. Debt may seem a way of life to most people, so it's possible that you might overlook that and not see it as a curse at all. Take a careful look at the debt in your past and see if it has been destructive in anyway. The debt in your past could have been the cause of many of your family's problems.

An example could be that there is a possibility that there is a long line of illness in your past, at the same time there is a great deal of debt. Take away the debt and you may eliminate a whole lot of illness because it's possible that the illness is caused by the anxiety that was caused by the debt. Am I starting to paint a colourful picture for you now? The entire aim of God wanting to bless you is so that you can bless others. He doesn't dare you to get blessed just so you can be blessed, He has a plan, He wants you to bless others and start a chain reaction in His kingdom.

When Satan tempted Jesus with all the world's wealth, He was only tempting Jesus with something He was about to become His anyway, and when it became Jesus' it also became ours because we are joint heirs with Jesus.

Radical Giving Unleashes God's Power

This was a real problem for Satan, as he never wants what's best for us. In Acts 2, radical giving began and thousands were added to the church daily. In Acts 4 the same thing was happening, and the people started laying money at the apostles' feet. Then in Acts 5, the enemy used the same tactics as he did in the garden. He got man and woman to agree. A withholding spirit was released into the foundation of the New Testament church, after Acts 5 until the end of revelation we find no account of radical giving, no account of thousands being added to the church daily.

This withholding church had legal authority in the foundation of the church. What does the withholding spirit make a play for? The tithe! This gives the devil authority in our lives because we release the withholding spirit in our lives. If we start giving and tithing, we break the curse of the withholding spirit. We can't bring the correction to our financial situation until we bring the solution. This solution is to deny power to the withholding spirit, thereby become joint heirs again with Jesus Christ.

The dictionary's definition of debt is: Money owing, arrears, liability, debit, balance, balance due, and obligation. The Bibles also has instructions as far as debt is concerned.

"Settle matters quickly with your adversary who is taking you to court. Do it while you are still with him on the way, or he may hand you over to the judge, and the judge may hand you over to the officer, and you may be thrown into prison. I tell you the truth, you will not get out until you have paid the last penny."

- **Matthew 5: 25-26**

If you have incurred a debt, settle it as quickly as possible. God warns us as to how far debt can go. It's not just a simple case of the dictionary definition on the previous page, but it leads to so much more. In today's day and age, if you can't pay your debt, you are likely to lose that which you can't pay for. In Jesus' days you were thrown into jail if you couldn't pay your debt and weren't let out until each and every penny was paid for.

I think it might have been a more effective system then, you would have thought twice before incurring a debt – the consequences were greater than today. I firmly believe that God's desire is for us to live a debt free life. He has even made provision for us in his law so that we don't spend the rest of our lives in debt.

No Debt for More Than Seven Years

"At the end of every seven years you shall grant a release of debt. And this is the form of the release: Every creditor who has lent anything to his neighbour shall release it; he shall not require it of his neighbour or his brother, because it is called the

Lord's release. Of a foreigner you may require it; but you shall give up your claim to what is owed by your brother,"

- **Deuteronomy 15:1-3**

It was not God's plan that we would be in debt. God put this arrangement in Deuteronomy, into his law, so that no one would remain in debt for more than seven years.

What you do today for the sake of tomorrow is called investment, what you do at the expense of tomorrow so you can enjoy today, is called debt. Be encouraged and take a step in the right direction by starting to invest rather than living in the bondage debt. If you don't get the giant, the giant will get you! So deal with it as soon as you can.

As soon as he broke his stewardship role with His Father he was put outside of the garden. And his disobedience caused his blessings to be lost because of this.

Even today, our unseen enemy is still trying to insist upon that curse that was broken 2000 years ago upon the cross. We should not be walking in poverty anymore as we have come into that relationship of stewardship again through Jesus Christ.

Our Struggle Is Not Against Flesh And Blood

"For our struggle is not against flesh and blood, but against the rulers, against the authorities, against the powers of this dark world, and against spiritual forces of evil in the heavenly realms."

- **Ephesians 6:12**

These who are not 'flesh and blood' are demons over whom Satan has control. They are not mere fantasies – they are very real. We face a powerful army whose goal is to defeat Christ's church. When we believe in Christ, these beings become our enemies, and they try every device to turn us away from Him and back to sin.

Although we are assured of victory, we must engage in the struggle until Christ returns, because Satan is constantly battling against all who are on the Lord's side. We need supernatural power to defeat Satan and God has provided this by giving us

His Holy Spirit within us and his armour surrounding us. If you feel discouraged, remember Jesus' words to Peter. "On this rock I will build my church, and the gates of Hades will not overcome it"

This scripture can be applied to every area of our lives, including finances. The giant in this chapter cannot be killed with five smooth stones. This battle needs to be fought with a careful balance of physical and spiritual warfare. We may find that God wants us do physical things to symbolize what He wants to do in the spiritual. For example, you will need to actually pay your tithe physically into the tithe basket to break the curse and receive the blessing. You can't only pray about these things you need to take action at the same time.

Also, in order to break the generational curses that you may find, you will need to pray and possibly enter into some spiritual warfare. In Ephesians 6:12, we realize that we are fighting four different levels of spiritual powers. Tackling principalities is of no use because they have the legal right to be there. In order to remove their power we need to become obedient to God, then the principalities will fall away because they have no right to be there anymore. As we free our tithes and offerings, they become weapons of destruction against the powers of darkness.

Through His Poverty You Might Become Rich

"For you know the grace of our Lord Jesus Christ, that though He was rich, yet for your sakes He became poor, so that you, through his poverty, might become rich."

- **2 Corinthians 8: 9**

This scripture can mean many things, but the Greek in Strong's concordance #4433 is *'Ptocheuo'*. To be destitute, poor as a beggar, reduced to extreme poverty. The word suggests the bottom rung of poverty, a situation in which one is lacking in things of this world.

This clearly refers to it in financial terms and I believe that amongst other things, Jesus took our poverty on the cross, so that we might become rich. If this is so, we must also realize that we can't engage God's financial system using the world's principles and standards. We must choose one system and one system only. You can't expect and claim God's blessing while you are using the world's system for gain as well. It's one or the other, kind of like mixing oil and water. No matter how hard you try, they just don't go together.

We Are Not Of This World

"I do not pray that You should take them out of the world, but that You should keep them from the evil one. They are not of the world, just as I am not of the world."

- **John 17:15-16**

I am sure that Jesus didn't pray, "They are not of the world, just as I am not of the world" to inform His Father of this fact and I am quite sure that He didn't need to remind himself either. I believe that this was prayed as a reminder to us, we are not of the world and it's vital that we keep this in mind when tackling our financial issues.

It is so easy to get caught up in the things of this world that we can easily forget that we are not of this world. What good is it for us to be just the same as those that are of the world? We have to be different in so many ways and I believe that we can be different in our approach to financial matters. There have been many opportunities in my life to share the gospel simply because my finances were handled *differently*.

It often starts by, "Why do you give so much to the church?" or "How do you survive on such a small income?" The response to these questions is always – GOD! There is no other logical way to explain how we live off of what we do and why we spend our money so differently to others. As Christians we have to be focused on God at all times and not on our next purchase. It is sad to see how so many people depend on their next purchase for their joy!

I too love getting new things and enjoy shopping; there is no crime in that. The crime is when we *need* to buy to make us happy, when our hope is in the next payday. This lifestyle is never satisfying and that is why those who live like this need debt – there is just never enough money to buy joy.

God's Nature Is to Bless

Jesus had the victory and it's ours for the taking. We will do the same as Jesus did and greater things also! Our finances can be used as spiritual weapons. We are in a spiritual battle, so we've got to use the right weapons otherwise we are not going to make any impression in this conflict. If David put on armour and took the sword, Goliath would have slaughtered him. He knew what weapon he needed to be using and despite the advice of a whole army, he stuck to his conviction and defeated Goliath.

God's nature is to bless, but Satan has come to kill, steal and destroy. Let's use our God given weapons and win the battle. In fact, it's already been done, so what's all the fuss about? Simply claim it in Jesus' name. First and foremost, if you want success, then *listen* to the one who designed you for success. It is difficult to know what to do and how to do it with your finances. Ask God to give you a conviction concerning your finances, after all God doesn't work from a recipe so my conviction will not be yours. I may have a conviction to give 25% of my income to the poor and needy, but you may be called to invest your money in Stocks and Bonds so that in 10 years time when God asks, you will have the cash necessary to plant a new church. God may also be calling you to save diligently because in three years time He wants you to open a business that will make you hugely wealthy so that you can support the local AIDS clinic financially.

Not one of us know for sure what God has in store for us, and He can only do it if we listen to Him and stick to our conviction. There was a time when I had a substantial amount of money available to me on a monthly basis and I had no idea why. (I have realised over the years that God generally has a plan when He gives you money.) I prayed about it and felt that God was saying that I should use some of the money to purchase much needed goodies for my house and then give the rest to a family that was struggling. Throughout the months that followed I was tempted to use the money for many other things but when it came to the crunch, I had a conviction and stuck to it.

If I didn't have that conviction I may have gone off on a tangent of some sort and achieved none of what God wanted me to. When you stick to your conviction there is a certain peace that comes with it. I would rather live in that peace than have ten times my salary and always feel empty. I reckon Satan hates God given conviction so use it for your own good and as a weapon against the enemy

Chapter 5

For Such a Time as This

For Such a Time as This

Claiming the covenant

"Reasonable men adapt themselves to their environment. Unreasonable men adapt their environment to themselves; therefore all progress depends upon the efforts of unreasonable men."

George Bernard Shaw

Esther was called by God to proclaim a particular message at a particular time. The time was of the utmost importance and so was the message. If Esther had not been obedient, the history of the Jews would have been completely different. Her message and timing was pivotal to the Jews and because of Queen Esther's obedience and courage, a whole nation was saved. In the same way, I feel strongly that this is the time that the church should rise up and take hold of the covenant and promises that are ours. We have been asleep for far too long, and a great responsibility awaits us. The covenant needs to be claimed now and applied by all Christians all over the world.

Now is the time for Christians to fight for the economy of the land and for the wealth of their nation. I believe God is going to rise up 'Esthers' in each nation to proclaim a bold message that is ripe and ready for this season. We are going to take back the land and posses it. We are going to fight for our dominion and not sink back and ignore the mess that the world has got into! Christians now is the time!

Firstly, it needs to be absolutely clear that we need to claim and proclaim this message for the sake of the gospel – our very purpose for being alive. Should we stray from that purpose and become self-seeking and self-serving, we will lose out on the blessing that God has in store for us. I believe that we can never truly be satisfied with our financial situation if it is merely for us to lead a comfortable and blessed life. There has to be more than that, there has to be a purpose! The number one message for our time, the end time church, should be:

Prosperity with a Purpose

I don't believe that Jesus or His disciples were poor. I have heard many arguments both for and against the fact that He wasn't poor, but the evidence that I have heard for Jesus and His disciples not being poor is more convincing than the evidence against this. I believe Jesus lived the life that we should try and live. He is our role model. GOD WANTS US TO PROSPER! **Here's proof from the word.**

" And you shall remember the Lord your God, for it is He who gives you power to get wealth, that He may establish His covenant which He swore to your fathers, as it is this day."

- **Deuteronomy 8:18**

Strongs # 3581 Power, 'koach' (ko-akh); Vigour, strength, force, capacity, power, wealth, means or substance. Generally the word means 'capacity' or 'ability', whether physical, mental, or spiritual.

Here Moses informs Israel that it is God who gives to them the ability (power, means, endurance, capacity) to obtain wealth, for material blessings are included in the promises to the patriarchs and their descendants. Moses strictly warns Israel in verse 17 not to falsely conclude that this capacity for success is a natural talent, but to humbly acknowledge that it is a God-given ability.

Prospered to Bless

Prosperity exists to establish and confirm the covenant. It should not be squandered selfishly. God's desire is for us to not only have our basic needs met but He also wants us to live in abundance. On top of that, He wants us to have our heart's desires. So what do we do with all this abundance, do we store it away for safekeeping? Of course not! God desires that we use our abundance to bless others. God's covenanted prosperity is always a means to an end and never an end in itself.

"Beloved, I pray that you may prosper in all things and be in health, just as your soul prospers."

- **3 John 2**

God wants us to have abundance but this is not limited to money. A person can have millions and still be poor: poor in health, poor in peacefulness, and poor in relationships. Wealth is more than money and possession. We need the wisdom both to receive God's covenant of prosperity but to receive wealth without it controlling us. We also need to see that with wealth and health, peace and friendship – we <u>serve others.</u>

It is clear that God wants His children to prosper. How can anyone deny that? However, prosperity should not be the end in itself. It ought to be the result of a quality of life, commitment, dedication, and action that is in line with God's Word.

Prosper in Greek is *'euodoo'* and literally means, 'to help on the road' or 'succeed in reaching'. It clearly implies that divine prosperity is not a momentary, passing phenomenon, but rather it is an ongoing progressing state of success and well-being.

It is intended for every area of our lives; the spiritual, physical, emotional and the material. However, what God does not want is to unduly emphasize any one area. We must maintain a balance.

"The thief does not come except to steal and to kill and to destroy. I have come that they may have life, and that they may have it more abundantly."

- **John 10:10**

As you give all of who you are to God, God in turn gives all He is to you. God's covenant to us is a covenant for abundant life. From the very beginning of time, Scripture shows us that God wanted us to be happy and prosperous. In Genesis we are told that God made everything and declared it to be good. Then He gave this beautiful, plentiful earth to Adam; Adam was given dominion over all of it (Genesis 1:28). God's plan from the beginning was for man to be enriched and to have a prosperous, abundant life. Here Jesus declared His intention to recover and restore to man what was the Father's intent and to break and block the devil's intent to hinder our receiving it.

Your first step toward experiencing full biblical prosperity is to believe that it is God's highest desire for you. The next step is to line up your highest desires with God's will for you.

It is very sad to see that so many of us are settling for the bare minimum, we are happy as long as we are keeping our heads above water. Very few people are reaching for success. We have developed a maintenance plan in our minds that dulls the pain of life but does not reach for the stars. How often do we not admire those that are at the top and call them lucky? We all want what they have, some of us mimic their behaviour, other simply envy them and one or two people have formulated a seven-step program to be just like them.

It is so simple for us to focus on the wrong thing, to try copy every aspect of the successful, to try our best to be like them, live like them and act like them. We create an icon out of them and study the so-called recipe of success. Would it not be better to get to the heart of the matter, the real issues, the inner working of such an existence?

How many of us accept one hundred percent the lot we have been given. I guess very few of us, and why? Again I guess it's because we believe that there has to be more out there. We have all been designed to live a life of abundance and of excellence.

Shaping Our Future

As we begin to look inward and learn about ourselves we see that we can shape our future and have an influence on our very own lives. The buck does stop with us. If we are struggling financially it may be because we are not doing one of many things that we should be doing. When I went through a ten-year period of financial difficulty I also came out of it realizing that I could change my circumstances. I learnt to accept that God was in control but my attitude to the struggles had a huge effect on their outcome. I also learned to use what God had given me. God gave me a hard time, was I going to curse Him for it or see what He would do in that time. That time to me was more valuable than any amount of money.

I learned valuable life lessons, especially financial ones. When the hard times did eventually end, I could see that they were necessary and my life had taken a completely different course because of them. I knew that I was going to experience much abundance because of the hard times that I had experienced. In the time that we were flat broke I never despaired, I knew that there was more out there. There was something deep down inside that screamed out for more and fought to get to the more. It wasn't a fight for more money; it was a fight for more life! I knew with all my heart that there was more to life than this.

If you are a person who is reaching for success, be careful not to reach for more money. If that's all you are reaching for then you will be disappointed when you get it. Reach higher and dig deeper, life has so much to offer! There are two kinds of people in this battle, the people that give up and the people that push through. They carry on. Which one are you? Are you reaching for the stars or have you quit?

God Wants To Bless Us

I believe that God wants to bless us far more than we want to be blessed ourselves. A large part of our financial worries is about freedom. How many times do you see adverts on television, radio, billboards, and etc "Financial freedom is yours! You can be free from debt! Attend this course to teach you how to be financially free." It is true, you can be financially free but it is not at all what the world advertises. It is hard work to get to a place of financial freedom, and I don't mean the kind of work that you do from nine to five. It is more a decision kind of work. You need to change your mindset and change what you term free.

Does free mean having no debt and enough money to live comfortably, or does free mean to have an inner freedom, a genuine peace that permeates your everyday life. I was more financially free when I was down and out with no money than when I had plenty. When I was down and out I was forced to take a fresh look at life and re-evaluate so many things. I see myself as privileged to have been able to do that and many of you may never get that opportunity which might make it even harder for you. It is easier to face these issues when you have to, when life's circumstances give you little option.

The hard part is when you have plenty and need to re-evaluate your life and make changes with no pressure, just your own decision and conviction. When I had no money I could only depend on God but when I had money I had the added responsibility of using my own wisdom and initiative but at the same time still needed to depend on God. Do you have any idea how hard it can be to depend on God when life is going so well?

It is hard because you are fooled into believing that you are self-sufficient and may begin to neglect God. Freedom is realising that you always need God, living life to the fullest whether rich or poor and having the highest regard for God's every word. If He says to you, give a million pounds away, and you only have ten pounds it should be as easy as if you had the million pounds to give away in the first place, because you do and that's the freeing part. All God's resources are available to us and no matter what circumstance we find ourselves in we need to be free in that very fact.

Dads Know Best

God has given us so many Scriptures to prove that He desires for us to be blessed. His heart is filled with a Father's love for His children and what dad doesn't want to see his children have all the great things that he can offer. The one thing we must remember about dads is that they know what is best for their children! A child may demand sweets, insist that they need sweets and have a good case in favour of them having sweets.

Only the father knows that the child would have rotten teeth very soon if she continued to eat sweets. The dad who understands this danger has to say no from time to time. Our Dad, Father God, is just the same, He knows what we need and He knows what's best for us. We really need to rest in that and trust Him completely. Right from the very beginning, God set out to *spoil* us, to give us the crème de la crème, the cream of the crop, the best in life. The Garden of Eden was the best and we blew it. God didn't give up; He spoke to Abraham and instituted a covenant that would ensure that we were blessed.

COVENANT: agreement, contract, convention, treaty, promise, and pledge.

The Abrahamic covenant of blessing was established and this was God's way of helping us back into His blessings. This covenant was established four hundred and thirty years before the law was written. It was not the law. The very base of this covenant was the tithe. We need to **start here** with the tithe if we want to start the process of freedom, to re-establish or form the Abrahamic covenant of blessing in our lives. Firstly, we need to agree to the covenant in order for it to be effective. If there's no agreement, then there is no contract.

As you saw above, a synonym of covenant is agreement. All we really need to do here is agree. Secondly, we need to obey the terms and conditions laid out in the covenant/contract or else we will be forced to forfeit. For example, if you don't make your car payments your car will be repossessed. In this section, we need to know our Bible, we need to be tithing, etc. And thirdly, there has to be a trade of something or it's not a covenant. Back to the car example, you give cash and for that cash you get a car. We need to give our lives to the plans and purposes of God and He will give us covenant blessings. Part of the covenant blessing is so that we can bless. If we are in this for the money and not for the plans and purposes of God, we will fall short and miss the mark completely.

If we are not familiar with the terms and conditions of the covenant, Satan is quite likely to pounce on you and rob you of the blessing. He is waiting to find a loophole in this contract so that he can step in and rob you. Remember, he has very little function on this planet. His primary reason for being here is to kill, steel and destroy[12] and if you are a born again child of God, you are his primary target.

Most Christians today use the excuse that the tithe is in the Old Testament and does not apply today, but this is not the case. The tithe is a covenant. When the law came about, four hundred and thirty years later, after this covenant was established, it became part of the law. It went through the law and then came out of the law through grace because Jesus died on the cross and gave us the opportunity to live by grace through faith. At this point, it stopped being law again.

I want to encourage us to consider the importance of the covenant and the blessings that we are entitled to through the covenant that was instituted in the Old Testament before the law. The covenant that God gave to Abraham is the covenant that we should claim back into our lives today.

"The Lord had said to Abram, "Leave your country, your people and your father's household and go to the land I will show you. I will make you into a great nation and I will bless you; I will make your name great, and you will be a blessing. I will bless those who bless you and whoever curses you I will curse; and all peoples on earth will be blessed through you. So Abram left, as the Lord had told him; and Lot went with him."

- **Genesis 12:1-4**

Five times God speaks of Abram being blessed, I think it's extremely clear what He meant, He wanted Abram blessed, I don't think that there is a hidden meaning – He wanted to bless Abram and He wanted other people to bless Abram," I will bless those who bless you and whoever curses you I will curse"

There is no need to dispute the very basic desire of God's heart here. It's very clear that He wanted to bless us. It wasn't only for Abram, because the last part says," and all peoples on earth will be blessed through you". God made provision in Abram's promise for all the people of the earth, which includes you and I today. This raises a question, why are many of us not blessed.

Cash the Cheque

The first step to access the blessing of the covenant is to claim it. If we get a cheque we have to go to the bank to cash it. It's no good sitting with it in our wallets for the rest of our lives - we must cash that cheque. In Abram's case, he wasn't able to cash the cheque just yet; he had to do what God said first in Genesis 12:4, "So Abram left, as the Lord had told him". Abram was obedient and it is possible that we are lacking that first vital step - obedience. If we are going to claim the blessing then we must first check if God has asked us to do anything for Him. In Genesis 15:1-19 God makes a legal declaration and confirms the covenant with Abram. There is a legal contract between God and us stating that he (and the rest of us) will be blessed.

Unfortunately, God took a little too long for Abram and he thought that God meant he should help Him a little, so Ishmael was conceived. How often do we do this, we try to help God! Is it because we don't trust Him, or maybe we think we heard wrong in the first place, or maybe we just think that God cannot actually do it? Folks, God is true to His word and unfortunately it very seldom happens in the time frame that we want it to. We are still God's children and in a childlike manner we want it immediately, even though we think we are being mature about it.

If we are ever going to walk in covenant blessing, we should stop making other plans to help the original plan along. Trusting God completely, even if it doesn't look like it is ever going to happen, is the key. I am not preaching at you here, I know how it feels. I have spent ten years of my life waiting for God's promises to be fulfilled in my life. I still haven't seen the full blessing, nowhere near what He has promised. It took me ten years to get to the Jordan River and then to begin to move across it into the Promised Land. It's all a journey and we have to be patient and walk the journey in obedience and with faith.

I have noticed that God is extremely clever. I look back over the last ten years and see all the times that the blessing just wouldn't have been good for me. The lessons that I have learned along the way have been so valuable and I can see how God has been moulding me and shaping me to be able to contain this promise.

If I had the covenant blessing at any point over the last ten years, it would have all disappeared by now and I might have been in some serious trouble. I was not able to contain that blessing or manage it properly, I would have cracked and leaked it all out and no one would have benefited.

You can never assume that you are ready, if you think you are ready then it's quite possible that you are not really ready at all. If you are trying to hurry God up then you are far from ready. If you are trying to help God out, then you are even further from ready. God's timing is all part of the blessing. He is more than capable of giving whatever He wants to us at any point of our life. And we should be at peace and be grateful that He loves us so much that He only does the very best for us. Again in Genesis 17:1-27 God confirms the covenant with Abram and his descendants. God made very sure that we understand that He wants us to be blessed. He makes sure that we understand. It was very necessary for Him to go over the contract a few times so that we could understand all the details. First of all, it is legal and binding.

Secondly, there is a God part and a man part – Abraham had to circumcise all the males so that God could bless him. How much more could a man want? What God was offering far outweighed what He wanted in return, yet I think that if we didn't have to give anything in return, there would have been no accountability and no contract? Then it would just have been God giving and us taking. This way we have a binding contract with God.

"If you belong to Christ, then you are Abraham's seed, and heirs according to the promise."

- **Galatians 3:29**

It's that simple, the proof that we are entitled to the promise. If we are obedient then God will bless us. The Bible says it in black and white, no interpretation necessary. If you belong to Christ, then you are Abraham's seed, and heir according to the promise. But just in case you are not convinced I have a little more proof for you to consider. The tithe will do the following in the area of your finances:

1. Protect

"And I will rebuke the devourer for your sakes, So that he will not destroy the fruit of your ground, Nor shall the vine fail to bear fruit for you in the field," Says the Lord of hosts;

- **Malachi 3:11**

Random disasters that rob you of your finances stop happening such as illness and car breakdowns because you are protected by God.

God wants to rebuke the devourer for our sakes but too often He is unable to do so because of our disobedience. Sadly, statistics show that eighty percent of the church is robbing God and then that eighty percent wonders why their finances aren't blessed.

2. Position

"And all nations will call you blessed, for you will be a delightful land," Says the Lord of hosts.

-   **Malachi 3:12**

Tithing began in Genesis where Melchizedek received Abram's tithe after he had won a great battle. It was an act of great gratitude for what God had done for Abram. It cannot be coincidence that Abram was the first person to give God a tithe and then he went on to be the founder and father of the entire nation of Israel.

Our tithe positions us. Our desire to give to God sets us up for what God desires to give to us. We cannot lose if we tithe but we will lose if we don't. Don't risk your entire future, your destiny just because you don't like to tithe. Position yourself through tithing and you will be blessed and will be a *delightful land*.

It's your choice as always, but why would you put yourself in a position where you know you will lose? Put yourself in a position to be blessed.

3. Multiply

"Bring all the tithes into the storehouse, that there may be food in My house, and try Me now in this," Says the Lord of hosts, "If I will not open for you the windows of heaven and pour out for you such blessing that there will not be room enough to receive it."

- **Malachi 3:10**

Money reveals your true nature. God will always test how you handle money and will increase your money according to your ability to handle it. In Genesis 22 God tested Abraham with Isaac. Even though he had just given the first tithe ever, God needed to test him.

Is what you are facing now a test? Is it the test that will come directly before the great multiplication that God has planned for you? Are you perhaps being tested with the very thing that God has blessed you with? Abraham was given a son and then asked to sacrifice his son.

Tithing positions you for so much blessing that you will not have room enough to contain it. Abraham received an entire nation!

Once we have obediently tithed we can expect blessings to result. Sometimes they simply appear and other times you have to make a withdrawal from your heavenly account. Here are some suggestions on how to access your blessings.

Ask

"Ask and it will be given to you…"

-   **Matthew 7:7**

"But even now I know that whatever You ask of God, God will give You."

-   **John 11:22**

Ask in Jesus name

"If you ask anything in my name, I will do it"

-   **John 14:14**

Whilst writing this book, I suddenly had a panic attack! I thought that if I want to publish this book, I have to have a testimony as a base to share from. How many people are going to believe what I am saying if I am still in the deepest of poverty? I know that I believe every word that I have written and I know that I have applied all that I write and as far as I know I have been obedient to God. I can't think of anything that I have not tried or applied in this area, in order to have victory, yet we continue to struggle financially.

Lord, what do you want from me, help? I can't help other people if I have no evidence in my own life. While I was having this little tiff with the Lord at about 3am, He gently reminded me that I was writing this out of obedience and it was not up to me to convince anyone, it was up to me to be obedient. Then He asked this little question. Would I have written this book if I had not been in the position that I am in now? Would I have written this book if I had not lived all that I am writing and testifying to? The answer of course is no.

This book is the result of the life that I have led and the principles that I am sharing are principles that I live and believe. It's up to you to decide if you want to give it a bash and trust God no matter what. If God has promised me covenant blessings, then they will come and I have to rest in that and trust His timing. Almost two days after I had finished this very book, it happened! Opportunity knocked and my life of poverty ended – almost instantly.

How's that for timing? I was released into a new level of freedom, into a level of prosperity. I still wouldn't call that the Promise Land though, I believe that God has so much more for us in life and very few people get to the place where they have all that God wants them to have. I am certainly going to try to get there though – not so that I can be rich but so that I can do all that God wants me to do in this lifetime, whatever that may be!

Chapter 6
Sowing and Reaping

Sowing & Reaping

You can't have one without the other

This entire chapter is a beautifully illustrated sermon that was preached by the senior pastor of Fountain Vineyard Church, Dave Pederson from Port Elizabeth, South Africa.

I found the message so beautiful that I tried to change very little of it. Dave Pederson has a magical way of bringing the whole story of the five loaves and two fish to life. His every word is like the stroke of an artist's brush on a canvas that completely draws you into the story and brings it to life.

Apart from his brilliant storytelling, the message also comes across in a very powerful way. You can't read this and not have a new perspective on sowing and reaping.

He Saw a Great Multitude

Matthew 14:13-21 says, "When Jesus heard it, He departed from there by boat to a deserted place by Himself. But when the multitudes heard it, they followed Him on foot from the cities. And when Jesus went out He saw a great multitude; and He was moved with compassion for them, and healed their sick. When it was evening, His disciples came to Him, saying, "This is a deserted place, and the hour is already late. Send the multitudes away, that they may go into the villages and buy themselves food."

But Jesus said to them, "They do not need to go away. You give them something to eat."

And they said to Him, "We have here only five loaves and two fish."

He said, "Bring them here to Me." Then He commanded the multitudes to sit down on the grass. And He took the five loaves and the two fish, and looking up to heaven, He blessed them, broke the bread and gave the loaves to the disciples; and the disciples gave to the multitudes. So they all ate and were filled, and they took up twelve baskets full of the fragments that remained. Now those who had eaten were about five thousand men, besides women and children."

The Picnic with 5000 People

What an awesome picnic, imagine a picnic from five loaves and two fish with five thousand men besides women and children. Approximately twenty thousand people were fed on that day.

Matthew 14 is a wonderful passage, which really highlights the whole principle of sowing and reaping. We can look at this story from a number of different angles; however I want to look at it specifically from the angle of sowing and reaping.

Jesus needs time alone. It's lovely to see Jesus' humanity coming through. He's in touch with His emotions. He has had bad news, and He needs time alone. Even in the context of His time alone, He gets inundated with ministry needs and He doesn't respond in frustration and anger like some of us would want to do. He responds with compassion, and He listens to the Father's opportunism, He responds with the Father's power and heals the sick.

And then, in verse 15, His disciples come to Him and say, "look it's getting late. Let's organise this thing by sending the multitudes away!" But Jesus says in verse 16 that they didn't need to go away. His disciples had jumped to the wrong conclusion. The people had come for a purpose. They were there to hear them, the ministry was not completed, and this meeting was going to go on for a couple of days. They didn't need to go away.

"You give them something to eat." Jesus put the ball right back in His own disciple's court.

Management Training Dynamics

And that's a good management training dynamic, to train people not just by telling them, but also by exposing them to opportunities. Do you know that you grow best by actually doing? You need to actually get out there and start *doing*. You can only retain so much by hearing it and by seeing it, but by doing it you get the maximum retention and comprehension. And so Jesus was giving His disciples firsthand experience on looking to the Lord, the Father, for His resourcefulness, His power, and His ability to provide. He says *you* give them something to eat. He encourages them.

And all that they could come up with was the little boy with the five loaves and two fish. I don't know how they managed to find the five loaves and two fish, but somehow they managed to get this little kid to bring his basket forward. Five loaves and two fish, that's all that they managed to get. And verse 18 holds the key, "Bring them here to me." Bring them to me, Jesus says. When we take what we have to Jesus, it is no longer just what it was; it becomes what it can be. When we keep what we have for ourselves, it will be what it was; enough for a boy to fill his stomach, and maybe if he's kind, a little bit for his buddy, but that's it.

But when we bring it to Jesus, what was good for one becomes good for twenty thousand. It's awesome and we don't know how it happens and I can take you through case after case in scriptures, where this is what happens. Let me give you two.

Elijah

In 1 Kings 17 there was a widow who needed a miracle of God for the feeding of herself and her son. And the prophet Elijah asked her to make him a meal. She took the last of what she had and yielded it to God to make a meal for the man of God. And as she did that, as she took the last of her flour, she found that a miracle took place. But she out of her faithful, sacrificial giving found that she herself never went without.

And there was always flour for her, right throughout that famine period of Elijah's life. And she always had enough for her and her son and she was able to meet all their needs because she brought what she had for the purposes of God.

Elisha

In 2 Kings 4 there's another similar incident with Elisha who was Elijah's disciple and it's interesting how often the miracles and the things that we've picked up from those that have gone before us in the Lord are the very things that God continues to accentuate and multiply in our own lives.

So Elisha had a similar experience where a woman who ran out of oil. As she took the last of what she had to serve him he told her to bring all her vessels and put them out. He then told her to begin to pour the oil into the empty vessels. And you know that the oil that she poured never ran out. The last of what she had she poured and it kept pouring, kept pouring. You see, it's when we take what we have, our little five loaves and two fish, and we bring them in that God causes the multiplication to take place. Why? Because of our faith. The whole principle of sowing and reaping is what it's all about. It's not just sowing something; it is sowing it in the name of the Lord. You know, if you are a farmer and you go and sow something in the wrong place at the wrong time you'll understand how stupid that can be.

It takes seed sown in the right season at the right place, in the right context and climate, and that can bring about a remarkable difference. So Jesus, in verse 19, brings the context to this miracle. He directs the people to sit down on the grass and He organises them, if you read the corresponding accounts in Mark and Luke, you'll see that He organises the people in groups.

The disciples get a bit of organisation going. Then He takes these five loaves and two fish and He begins to give them to the disciples. He didn't hand them directly to the people, He hands them to the disciples who in their very hands see the miracle take place. That's one of the great things of God; He loves for us to share the miracle out there, for more people to be involved. Jesus could have taken the bread and handed it to the people Himself. He could have said, OK, line up here, and He could have given it to the people Himself. But He doesn't, He takes it to the disciples, and He wants them to enjoy it.

Enjoy and Partake Of the Miracle

And I think He's saying the same thing to us, He wants us to enjoy and partake of the multiplication miracle that comes about through sowing and reaping. And so the disciples, having received this bread, get to give it to the people. Then it says in verse 20, they all ate and were satisfied. Now we wonder what happened between verse 19 and verse 20? Can you imagine being at that place? Could you imagine being there?

Jesus gives thanks. Holds the little picnic basket up to heaven and says, "Thank you Father for your power and your love and your resourcefulness." Then He calls the disciples and begins to give it to them. Even just for those twelve men to receive, there must have been a miracle that took place. I mean, between verse 19 and verse 20, between them receiving it and then imparting it to the others, the miracle of multiplication took place.

I wonder what you and I would have done had we been the disciples? We've just received it from the Lord, and it's a miracle, so we turn around and say to everyone, "Look everyone, it's a miracle, I'm going to eat it!"

But you see, they received a miracle to continue a miracle. They received something to impart it again, and again, and again. That's what happened. I don't believe that twelve disciples could have easily served five thousand men plus woman and children? How long would that queue have been?

But they could have gotten a pattern from Jesus and perpetuated that pattern.

A Miracle of Sharing

The people in turn gave it to a few others, who in turn gave it to a few others. What happened wasn't just a miracle of multiplication, but a miracle of sharing. And all the way along the line, each person had to make a choice. Do I eat this seed or do I sow it out again? They could have taken their little pile and eaten their little pile or they could have passed some on. And every bit that they passed on became enough for someone else, and someone else and someone else.

When I stop to think about it, I can see more into this because if it were I, I would have taken this thing, said thank you Lord and shouted, "Catch everybody!" then thrown it into the air and got out of the way as fast as I could. But Jesus did it; He had total trust in His Father. The food was enough for Jesus to have been well fed. Shouldn't the teacher be strong? Everybody could just have lay around and been weak because they were hungry, but the teacher must be strong because He's got to teach. You know that dilemma, you're in an airplane and there's only one parachute and three people, who should get the parachute? Well, it's the same in this story. There's only one picnic basket and five thousand people, who should get the food? Jesus should. He's the teacher, wouldn't you say? But He doesn't keep it to Himself; He immediately enters into the principle of sowing and reaping and sows it out. He doesn't eat his seed. When we come to know the Lord, we come, not because God needs us. Did you know that?

Generally we come to God when we're desperate, when we're needy. You know how much you need His cleansing, His forgiveness, His hope His power and truth in your life. And at the moment that you say, Father, I thank you for Jesus, I believe in Him, that moment, something happens. You are declared righteous before God. From that moment, God never looks at you as a dirty, rotten, condemned sinner. God looks at you with total acceptance, because at that moment, the righteousness of Christ is put upon your life. And you are justified and are at peace with God from then on.

Peace by Position

Now notice that the peace from God does not come because of the victories in your life, because of your accomplishments, how good you are or the good deeds you've done. Your peace comes because of your faith in Jesus Christ. But can I say for those of you who have never experienced it, it is a line you cross, an experience that you come into. It doesn't happen to some and not to others. It happens to all who believe. The gospel is the power of God unto salvation for all who believe. If there is not belief then there will not be true peace either.

I am not talking about religion; I'm talking about believing in Jesus. When it happens the righteousness of God is upon you, you are justified. And then the journey really begins because you have peace that is given to you by position. But you know what, when you are just going to walk out a life where you experience His peace in the daily battles of your life, you are walking in a process of sanctification. It's an ongoing journey. It's always on the foundation of justification so that we can never fail, and we are guaranteed to go to heaven one day.

But, the experience of heaven on earth and even the quality of our rewards in the life hereafter, depends very much on how much we have embraced the truths and the presence of God and the power of God in our lives. Even subsequent to our justification. I want you to see that there are three tenses to our being believers. The one is, *'I was saved and put my faith in Jesus Christ'*. In my case it happened many years ago, when I put my faith in Jesus Christ, I knew I had peace with God. It has never left me, but the life of living out His power, His truth, His presence, is a process of sanctification.

That process is going to be culminated and climaxed in what we call glorification, when Jesus returns. Upon His return, and He is going to return in the same way that He went for He said; "I will come back." And when He does come back, things will no longer be as they are. Instantaneously there will be a change. He will reign from that moment. He will reign, there will be judgement upon the earth and things that have been will no longer be. There will be transformation by the purging of fire as Peter says again and again in 1 Peter.

Another thing that is very significant upon His return is that we'll be glorified, our bodies will be transformed and we'll receive the same kind of body that Jesus has. He has already received His at His resurrection. His glorified body is what you and I can look back to as a prototype of what we will receive. Hebrews 2 says an interesting thing, it says, "Let's not neglect this great salvation." You see, our salvation is not about attending some evangelistic meeting, and signing on a pledge card about accepting Jesus. Our great salvation is not just about having peace with God as some fire insurance against hell.

Our salvation is much more. It's a life enjoying His transforming presence culminating in the final transformation which God will do instantaneously in us. Now what on earth has all that got to do with sowing and reaping? You see, this process of sanctification ending up in glorification is like the seed opportunity that we have to sow in righteousness to reap in mercy. Sow in God's ways, in God's purposes, to reap the harvest and have joy.

Enemies of The Cross

And though we might sow in tears, we are going to reap in joy. And it's the life that God has given us to use to sow out, not for our own pleasures, and that's the challenge of it. We're often tempted to take and eat our own five loaves and two fish. But God is saying that we need to sow it, will you spend this life sowing it for God's purposes or are you going to use this life for your own desires, your own appetites?

These are enemies of the cross of Christ, says Paul, whose God is their belly; they live only by natural instinct and desire. Who glory in their shame, who don't look to the glory of Christ in their life! Who glory in the things of which they should be ashamed! We need to see these things because if we don't we'll continue in our old patterns. And if we do what we've always done, we'll get what we've always got.

This is a straightforward business principle. The patterns that you have adopted in your organisation are perfectly suited to bring about the results that you are receiving right now. This is also true of our own lives, as a church, and it's true of us as a part of the body of Christ in the city as a whole. If we want something different, we have to set our eyes on a harvest that is different from what we have now. Then we need to sow seeds that are heading towards that harvest.

Sowing is Risky Business

Let me give you some truths about sowing. The first thing we need to see about sowing is that it is **risky business**. It was risky for Jesus and it was risky for the disciples to take what they had and to give it all away. It would have been safer to at least have Jesus and His disciples eat first. Let them be strong. If there are still some who are weak, who can't walk home later, then at least there are twelve who can help carry. It is risky to sow out there. It's risky for a farmer to take some of his seed and to sow it back into the soil. And to run the risk of losing it because anything can happen to it.

The rain might not come. Harvest might be delayed or ruined. Food might not be enough to last though the waiting period until the harvest. So it's risky, you can eat for a day on that seed or you could eat for a season from a harvest. But that's the risk, so do you wait for the harvest or do you eat the seed?

The Gospel of Luke has an interesting story on how you can move your assets from earth to heaven. Do you know how you can do that, because there's no removal company that will do that for you? I heard of a rock star that was so enamoured with his possessions that he stated in his will and had it read before they could bury him, that when he died they needed to bury him in his favourite Cadillac, with all his jewellery and everything in it with his favourite music playing. And they had to do that. A big grave was dug and his car was loaded into it with a crane and he was buried in it. You can't go to heaven in a Cadillac!

The reality is that we can't send our possessions on by any earthly means. There is only one way you can get your assets from earth to heaven. Do you know how you can do that? You find out where heaven is on earth and you sow into that.

If you wanted to move your money from this country off shore, and there weren't telecommunications and suitable facilities available you would have to use an ambassador. A portion of that other country in your country, and invest through that person. This would accrue to you as a benefit on the other side. So what you do in terms of Biblical principle here is you find the concerns of God, you find the concerns of heaven upon the earth and you put all that you are and have into that and it accrues to your account in the other land.

Every time we don't do that, every time we use what we have with carelessness, we carve out the concerns of God. We set them aside. We become too concerned about our own things, our own survival, ambitions, pleasures even our own anxieties.

What we're saying is, "Lord, I am not sending any of this to heaven. You can make heaven do with what you want to, but this is for me!" Do you know that is only going to go as far as three score and ten years, or whatever God might give you and that's where it's all going to end. Like the Cadillac in the ground, it'll go no further. So it's risky... sowing is risky because you are sending it on and not enjoying it now because you are choosing to eat for a season later rather than for a day now.

Like Esau whose brother Jacob, persuaded him, "do you want to have our father's pleasure, blessing and prosperity on your life for generations to come or do you want a meal now?" He said; "I want a meal now!"

"Is it worth your birthright?" Jacob said. "Yes it is." And Esau signed over his birthright to his brother for the sake of one meal. One meal, he threw away the harvest of generations of blessing and prosperity, he threw it all away because he was hungry that day. He threw away his future for one meal.

We wouldn't think very much of farmer who said: "Forget next year's harvest, I want to have a feast now. There's no need for sowing for the future!"

Sowing is risky.

In John chapter 12 Jesus says, "Except a grain of wheat fall on the ground and die, it remains alone, but if it dies, it bears much fruit." Jesus was talking about himself and about those who would come in His way and walk in His way.

We would also be like Him - He was the first fruit. We too would have to learn the way of living by dying. Then as we die, He says, we don't remain alone. Much comes. The seed is so that in one acorn can exist a whole forest of oak trees. But if that acorn is taken and set on a mantelpiece, and not put in the soil where it needs to be, and not nurtured as a seed sown with an expectation of a harvest, it remains alone. But if it's taken and sown it can bring forth a radically different thing, completely different from what we've been used to or expected. I just want us to know clearly that sowing is risky and we are not trying to take that away in any sense.

When Luther was being challenged in his trial about his commitment to the truths he had seen, his opponents trying to persuade him to recant, asked if he would die for what he believed or should they get a priest so that he could confess and recant. Luther said, "I would like to die in the faith by which I have lived." Luther understood that he was being challenged with the opportunity of saving his own skin and preserving the status quo or letting his life and ministry be a seed sown.

And you and I are here today in thankfulness for that seed that was sown. A seed that revived a fresh understanding of the gospel of grace that was lost in the dark ages. The seeds of men like Luther, brought about the harvest of millions of people.

Sowing Requires Timing

You want to sow at the right time as sowing takes time. You have got to stop other things in order to give time to the sowing. Hosea chapter 10 says, "It is time to break up your fallow ground, to seek the Lord and to sow in righteousness."

The other thing about timing and sowing is that not only does it take time to sow, but also *sowing requires waiting*. One of the ways you spell faith is W-A-I-T. It's an expectation that God will do it, but I have to wait for it. Many of us think that faith is spelled D-O-N-E but sometimes God wants us to wait. And that's part of what sowing is all about.

And of course there's also the actual expectation of reaping, and it takes time to reap. Sowing, waiting, reaping, all these things take time. And the harvest comes out of the sowing; it comes out of the time we spent in sowing. If we didn't take the time and the trouble to sow because we are so busy running around doing our own thing, we would lose the benefit of next year's harvest. Sometimes we don't get a harvest, not because we didn't have the courage to sow, but because we didn't take the time to prayerfully do that. We just didn't take the time to get down to it. And the challenge before us at this time is actually to say, Lord let me set the time aside. If it's time to pray, seek your face, time to weight up, time to work up how I can sow.

Galatians chapter 6:9 says, "Let us not become weary in doing good, for at the proper time we will reap a harvest if we do not give up."

Sowing Expresses Faith

I'm sure you're pretty clear on that. How could you take a little seed like the five loaves and the two fish, and even consider that this could be enough food for everybody? It takes faith.

You have to look beyond the circumstances through the eyes of faith. When Jesus looked at those five loaves and two fish, He saw five bakeries and a whole bunch of fishing boats.

It takes pivotal things to trigger new seasons and God wants to know whether we will be a people who walk in faith. Hebrews 11:6 says that "without faith it is impossible to please God, because anyone who comes to him must believe that He exists and that He rewards those who earnestly seek him." Faith is the only criterion in which you can please God.

Every change that takes place in your life for the better will come about not because you have been smarter than you were yesterday, but because you trusted God more today than you did yesterday. It comes as a result of trust. Will we be a people who sow in faith? Do we look through the eyes of faith? You know there's an old saying – God helps those who help themselves! Do you believe that? Well it never worked for me, every time I tried to help myself I ended up with egg on my face! After failing, I would humble myself and come to him and say, "Lord help me, because I can't help myself!"

He says, "I've been waiting for you to say that!" it's not true to say, God helps those who help themselves, in the humanistic sense. God helps those who trust him. We have to trust him in every action that we take. The reality is that even the strength we have to go to work each day comes to us from God. It's from God.

Paul says in Acts 17 that in Him we live and move and have our being. That's how we move from justification to glorification. By living in Him. Jesus said, the way we ought to do it is by abiding in Him, that's the word He used in John 15. Abiding in Him. Except we abide in Him we can bear no fruit.

Sowing Results in Thanks to God

And then I want to say to you lastly, that sowing results in thanks to God. And that is an amazing thing, when people can give thanks to God. They see the glory of God in something and they say, I want to know the God who enabled people to sacrifice and to sow to bring about a harvest like this. I want to know *that* God. Even atheists, when they are really grateful, are found to say, thank God! Story after story comes out of people who profess that they are atheist, and yet when they are really grateful, they end up saying, thank God!

There is something deep within the makeup of man that knows that God exists. And in our innermost being we know that the things that come to us that are good, ultimately come from God. In 2 Corinthians chapter 9:2, Paul says that sowing will result in thanksgiving to God. "Whoever sows sparingly will also reap sparingly, and whoever sows generously will also reap generously. Each man should give what he has decided in his heart to give, not reluctantly or under compulsion, for God loves a cheerful giver."

God is able to make all grace abound to you so that in all things at all times, having all that you need, you will abound in every good work. It goes on saying that in verse 11, you will remain rich in every way, so that you can be generous on every occasion and through us your generosity will result in thanks giving to God. And the next verses say the same thing. Ultimately, every act of true sowing and reaping will result in thanks giving to God.

It's because of the miracle of the power of the seed, like the five loaves and the two fish. Zechariah chapter 4 says that we should not despise the day of small beginnings. It's not by might nor by power, He says in the same chapter, but by my Spirit says the Lord. It's not by our might or our expertise, but it's by the power of the Spirit, that this strange vulnerable seed, this baby in a teenager's arm, in a backyard stable in Bethlehem becomes the saviour and the Lord of the world.

There was a man called Mordecai Ham, who was the Sunday school teacher to a man who went on to be the greatest evangelist of 2000 years of church history. He has preached to more people and seen more conversions under his ministry than anyone else and he's still alive today. His name is Billy Graham. Mordecai, his discipler and mentor, often thought to himself, "I thought I was wasting my life pouring into this kid and discipling this youngster. But look at him now!"

Mordecai is not alive anymore, but imagine his rejoicing as he looked at all those people accepting the Lord, being born again, being justified and starting the journey of walking in the presence of God and not outside of His presence.

Hebrews says that we are the people who have tasted the age of the powers to come. When the kingdom comes in fullness, it won't be any different from what we've begun to experience upon the earth. And if you don't like the taste of the kingdom that you've experienced, there's something wrong.

The Grace of God

Taste God and see that the Lord is good says the psalmist in Psalm 34. We need to get a taste of the goodness of God. Many of us have a taste of religion, a taste of obligation, of heaviness, manipulations. I want to move right away from all those things. I want God to give you a context for living your life. I want you to get a taste of God, the goodness of God.

Let's do what we're doing out of the sense of the goodness of God. It's awesome when that begins to come into reality for us. It changes things. Zechariah 4 says, it's not by might nor by power that mountains are moved, but by, my spirit. Secondly He says it's to the shout of grace and I want to declare grace over you. There's no obligation, there's no exclusion, there's no heaviness, there's just the grace that God gave us. As we understand the kingdom, we must understand the power of the spirit and the message of grace, the climate of grace of the favour of God. And if we have tasted His favour, we want to impart that to others, we don't want to look out of the crowd and tell them to find their own picnic. We want to take what we have and we want to share it. That's what grace does for us. True grace releases the little boy to give away his sandwiches. And then, it finally has to do with the power of the seed. Despise not the day of small beginnings. God would take your five loaves and two fish and multiply that to twenty thousand. That's awesome!

Chapter 7

Stewardship

Stewardship

Making it work

*Aim at Heaven and you will get earth 'thrown in':
aim at earth and you get neither. - C. S. Lewis*

Have you ever been so broke that you have no
petrol in your petrol tank (assuming you even have
a car) and no food to feed your children at the next
meal? Your phone is on the verge of being cut and
the car almost repossessed (just not quite because
the bank manager has given you another chance)?
School fees have not been paid at all in the last six
months and you still send your children to their
dance classes even though the teacher has not seen
an envelope with "fees" written on the front for
ages. In fact, she probably wonders if you are aware
that dance classes are not for free!

The children's school shoes have holes in them and they have worn the same school socks and shirts for the last three years. (You have to squash them into their uniform at times). New clothes have become a luxury, mending the old ones a lifestyle. Should I go on or do you get the picture?

This is the position that I found myself in during a particularly bad few years - broke and unemployed for the umpteenth time. Is this the abundant life that God has mapped out for me, I asked myself daily? It was Wednesday and on Monday of the same week Mo, found out that he had been retrenched and had two weeks left of his job. This was after working for the company for only three months. Before that it was about two years of working whatever odd jobs he could find.

It seems that in our ten years of marriage, we have had nothing but unemployment and poverty. Occasional moments of bliss did present themselves, but generally speaking, this was our life. It's a strange thing, but God has always been good to me. I had battled through most of my life and come out on top every time. Most importantly I have come out of my struggles gaining much more than money. The lessons that I had learned have given me richness in my life that no amount of money could ever have given.

Security during Financial Lack

Security was a reality in times of financial lack and peace the general state that I found myself living in despite the challenges. I wouldn't recommend this lifestyle for the faint hearted though. Despite this wonderful spiritual state of mind, there was still a reality out there and it was ouch! The situation was good and noble and I never discredited all the great works that God had done in our life, but there was still the nagging question that plagued me. "Isn't there more out there than this, am I called to a life of poverty for a greater spiritual cause or should I be trying harder?"

Was I to accept life as it was or try harder? That was the nagging question in the back of my mind constantly? Well, it was not as though I hadn't tried very hard, in fact quite the contrary; I had tried exceptionally hard in every possible way that I knew how.

It was at this point that I realised that there had to be more. Something just didn't sit right deep down inside my soul. I was totally convinced that I had not been called to be a 'Mother Theresa'. Some people are called to that and God gives them the grace to do it. I was more than willing to go that route, but God hadn't called me to that.

He had called me to live an abundant life and what I was living did not feel abundant at all. He had called me to be successful in the world, in business perhaps. He had not called me to be poor, but I was called to serve the poor. I began to meditate on all these things. He gave me clear instructions never to forget the poor. They would always be with us and I should be available to help them.

I became aware of patterns in the life of our family. I stayed home for many years to raise our children, but Mo seemed to be stuck in a never-ending cycle of:

Unemployed. Find work. Settle. Unemployed.

Lose it all. Find work. Settle. Unemployed.

Lose it all. Find work. Settle. Unemployed.

Lose it all... This was a vicious circle in our life and we had tried to break it in every way that we knew how. We prayed until the cows came home and tried to be obedient to God in every way. Still, the cycle continued. This led me to notice a few things.

A + B = C

A (A crossroad that we face)

+

B (The decision we make at that crossroad)

=

C (The outcome of **A + B)**

Or in other terms

A (The crossroad that we face)

+

B (The seed that we sow)

=

C (What we have reaped from our labour)

Principle of Cause and Effect

You can either live under cause and effect or you can use it. If you just want to live under cause and effect, then just live life and see where you end up. It's exciting, but very risky. You may end up where we were at the beginning of our journey. Or, you could take charge of your life and make cause and effect work for you! Now that's really exciting!! If you want cause and effect to work for you, you must know C. You must know the outcome of it. What do you want C to be? Ask God what He has to say about C. Once I had figured my sums out, I started to see the light. If I don't like what I get in C then I should change A + B.

Easier said than done, I know, but it was a starting point. I started to realise that we had followed patterns, without realising that they were patterns at the time. It started soon after our wedding day, we faced the first of our many cross roads. Mo was offered a job at a local nursery with a basic salary and all the security a job could offer.

At the same time his stepfather's firm gave him an opportunity to open a canteen for them in their factory. They would cover all the overheads (rent, electricity, etc) as well as provide a fully equipped kitchen. All we had to do was move in with our food, prepare meals and sell them to the local factory workers and other passersby in the surrounding areas.

Looking back, more than ten years later, I can see that the second opportunity was clearly a better opportunity than the first one, but you have to understand that when a man has to feed his wife and child, he generally opts for the more secure route. Much to our regret, we took the secure option and not the risky one, because we just couldn't be sure if the canteen would work.

Three months passed and the secure job ended. One of the men that worked under Mo as a trainee was given Mo's job, as the firm couldn't afford Mo a salary while the other man was willing to work for half the amount. Sadly, the lady that did take the canteen option was doing exceptionally well and had more work and income than she could cope with.

A+B=C Our C was back to A, back to unemployment again. After about nine months of casual work, (working in restaurants and bars) we hit a really rough spot, money was always tight and I guess that the pressure got too much. Mo and I separated. I moved out of town with our two-year-old daughter and Mo continued in our hometown. Once again, we ended up at C, this time our circumstances were even worse, we were separated **and** unemployed. Unfortunately fifty percent of today's divorces are a result of financial struggles. We were on the verge of being just another statistic.

Financial pressure in marriage is a destroyer, no matter how much you love each other, the pressure has to be released somewhere, and it often ends up coming out on each other. By the grace of God, we got back together after six months of a heartbreaking separation. Although our reunion seemed a good thing, financially, we were right back at A again but this time more determined than before to make a go of a good life.

After a string of casual jobs Mo finally got a job with a large catering firm. We had a degree of success there for almost three years, but again the pressure got too much as he was working night shifts and a great deal of overtime. It took its toll on us as a family, especially since we were expecting our second child. Mo began job-hunting again; fortunately this time he still had steady employment while he kept his eye out for greener grass.

A Brilliant Career Move

He found a great job and made a brilliant career move. The job was in the next town which was about forty minutes drive away, but that didn't seem too bad as the salary was so good. "Success" was beginning to taste good. This is where the testimony should have ended, a long and happy career at a good firm, but sadly it doesn't.

After another three years passed by, we found the pressure of travelling to the next town daily too much again and he began to look for work a bit closer to home. His daily routine was taking a toll on our family life again and we decided that it wasn't worth risking our marriage any longer. He used to get up at 5am to get to a train station in time to get to work and then he would only get home again as late as 9pm.

On a bad night he could get home as late as midnight. His children only ever saw him on weekends, sometimes. Our baby just never saw her daddy. It was a really hard time and we were miserable, so we took ourselves back to A. The job hunting started again and he took a job at the local fitness centre as a sales consultant. From a good salary and job security to a commission based job at a club where the staff turnover was high and the position was always risky. Now you must really think that we are completely stupid. I'm sure that you cannot understand why this chapter is called testimony.

The Pursuit of Happiness

What is the meaning of all this nonsense? We were desperately trying to find happiness. It just never seemed to be within our reach. We loved having time together as a family and found that we always had to choose between family and salary. We could never have both at the same time. Unfortunately this led us up and down these long winding paths of bad decisions and we continually ended up at point A, time and time again.

I guess, I don't need to tell you what happened next, we were back to the unemployment part of our cycle, still not realising that this was a vicious circle – a rut that we had to get out of. A wild frenzy of bad choices and stupid mistakes was the life that we had cut out for ourselves.

It seemed that we had gone too far and there was no turning back but also no going forward. We were stuck. The unemployment queue was becoming routine to us now. It wasn't too long before the sun shone again and Mo got a job as an insurance salesman managing a short term insurance book for a small firm. He was extremely happy with the firm as the working hours were perfect, really good for family life and he even came home for lunch occasionally, which was a real bonus. The first month went by and he didn't get paid his salary, but he loved the work, so continued in faith hoping that they would pay him shortly. A second month passed by and no salary was paid.

His employer assured him that he was going to get paid all that was due to him in due course. As you guessed, that day never came. Three months went by and he didn't see one penny in payment for his time. He was made redundant after the third month of no pay. Once again, back to A, back to the unemployment queues. The vicious circle was getting smaller; jobs and retrenchment were getting closer and closer to each other.

Once again another job and three months down the line, retrenchment reared its ugly head. Once again, the company could not afford the added staff. We spent months with no real income and lived by the grace of God. This is part of my testimony, but this is not the end of it, the real testimony only comes after the patterns have changed and the harvest is completely different. For now, I'll share a very significant part of our testimony though.

Provision through Burglaries and Brand New Shoes

For every penny we didn't have to meet our needs, we had friends whom God used to fill the gap, or an unusual circumstance that provided for us. I remember how we had an attempted burglary once; our home was broken into, but the burglars were disturbed and didn't manage to get away with anything. We didn't have a penny to our name but because of the attempted burglary, the landlord paid us to fit burglar proofing. The money that the landlord paid us for our labours in putting up the burglar bars paid for some food and put petrol in the car that weekend.

Another unfortunate situation was that our car was stolen from outside our property. This stirred up people in our church to give generously to us so that we could find a way to live without a car. Our car was recovered twenty four hours later and we were in a far better position than before the car was stolen.

I realise that this may not seem positive to you and it is not. No one wants to find provision through attempted burglaries and stolen cars. I have definitely seen the devourer at work but despite that I have seen God's redeeming power over my life. These stories are the extreme, but generally my life consisted of having my daily needs met one way or another, often food and money miraculously appeared in our times of need.

I remember a particular time when our daughter Lorah had worn right through her school shoes and there was no way we could replace them. It was quite embarrassing for her to have to go to school like that, but there was nothing we could do. Out of the blue a friend came to us with a brand new pair of school shoes for her. She said that she was given an unexpected bonus at work and thought of us and wanted to bless us.

The week prior to this she had seen Lorah at school and noticed her shoes. God really hears our cries and hearts desires. I often cried within at the way my children dressed. Although I was grateful that they had clothes I was a bit sad that it was not always the best clothes and so one particular day I mentioned this to God. Two days later, at our daughter's birthday party, she was given enough money to buy a few items of new clothing.

It was so special to just splash out on new clothes without any guilt, because the money was intended for her use and that's what she chose to use it for. Back to A+B=C, although this testimony is heart warming and it's so wonderful to see how God provides, it's not a lifestyle that anyone wants to lead all the time. No matter how much faith I have, I always find that it does take its toll on you eventually. It's hard, really hard! I don't know if I'm the only one who feels that way? The only real way that we have to get a different harvest is to sow different seeds, and so the journey began. As Albert Einstein said, "Insanity is doing the same thing over and over again and expecting different results." We would have been insane if we really expected to change the outcome but not change what we were doing!

It's easier said than done. What does it mean to sow different seeds and how do we put all this into practice. Where to from here?

First of all we identified certain patterns in our lives. The most apparent one to us was that we always took the safest routes when considering employment. Although this seemed like the responsible thing to do, for us it gave us a harvest of unemployment each time. What would it hurt to try a different route? Sow a different seed.

Secondly, we realised that we buckled under pressure too easily. We had been married for nearly ten years and decided that although family was still very important to us, we shouldn't let this be the factor that puts us out of work. A little sacrifice here and there may give us better rewards at another time.

We considered that if we sacrificed a bit of family time here and there and reaped a salary and accumulated some paid leave, we could reap a wonderful holiday together. This was something that we had not known at all because it was far too expensive for us to go away on a holiday.

There was a clear lack of a long-term plan. We had been living from day to day, payday to payday and our only real source of security was payday. Our only real aim was to reach the next payday.

These were the three main patterns that we picked up right away. We proceeded with extreme caution and prayed long and hard before taking a risky form of employment. The opportunity did present itself and at this point I need to make it quite clear that this is the route we had to take to change our patterns, I 'm not recommending that everyone do this.

Generally speaking, if you can hold down a good job and stay there your whole life, you've got it made. Work your way up the corporate ladder patiently and you will reap a good harvest. The examples given here are ones that we had to apply in order to reap a different harvest. I recently came across the following story, which sums things up beautifully.

"A middle-aged manager struggling to pay his bills, so he decides to get some advice from a financial expert.

The manager makes an appointment to meet with a well-respected financial advisor whose office was located in a swanky building on Park Avenue.

The manager enters the expert's elegantly appointed reception room, but instead of a receptionist, the manager is greeted by two doors, one marked "employed" and the other marked "self-employed".

He enters the door marked "employed" and is greeted by two more doors, one marked "make less that $40 000" and the other "makes more than $40 000".

He makes less than $40 000, so he enters that door, only to find himself face to face with two more doors. The door on the left is marked "saves more than $2000 a year" and the one on the right is marked "saves less than $2000 a year".

The manager only has about a thousand dollars in his savings, so he enters the door on the right – only to find himself back on Park Avenue!

The Same Doors Lead to the Same Results

It is painfully obvious that the manager in the story will never get out of his rut until he starts choosing to open different doors. The moral of the story is that most people are like the manager – they choose to enter the doors of life that lead them right back to where they started.

The only way for people to get different results is to choose to enter different doors, isn't that true? Like one of my mentors always used to say, "If you continue to do what you've always done, you'll continue to get what you've always gotten."

According to Business Week magazine, *"It takes the average worker half his lifetime to purchase a home, accumulate some savings and retirement benefits.   It takes about six months of unemployment to lose it all.*

We were at this place, having nothing. No home. No savings. No retirement benefits what so ever. So we took a job that offered a possibility of very high earnings in the near future, but they weren't guaranteeing anything, not even a basic salary, just commission. It was the hardest choice we ever had to make, especially after our long horrible track record of unemployment and poverty. I must add in at this point that changing what you are sowing may be extremely difficult. Human nature wrestles with change and always prefers the known route.

If you need to change patterns in your life, be careful. There are no guarantees what you will harvest and only at harvest time is the truth revealed. It makes sense though to assume that if you plant corn seeds, you will reap corn.

Another pattern that showed its ugly head in our monthly budget was a pattern of expenses exceeding our income and a lack of the ability to save. No matter how hard we tried, we never had excess to save. In the midst of all of this, our unemployment and poverty battle, I started thinking, "What do rich people do that I am not doing?" My motivation was to see if there was anything that I could do to help me get out of this rut of poverty.

The one thing that really stood out to me was that rich people had investments. They had savings, bonds, stocks, unit trusts, life insurance, education policies, etc. I began to ponder on this and I decided that I'm not going to say I can't anymore, but I am going to start. At least if I had a starting point I would be able to build on it.

Nothing plus nothing equals nothing, but if I took a small amount each month it would add up. It was a very hard thing to do for two reasons, first of all, finding the small amount of money was not easy because we already had more expenses than we did income, and this was just added to our expenses. Secondly, you won't believe how rude banks can be. I went to many financial institutions and they basically said that I should wait until I could afford it. It wasn't worth it for me to put such a small amount into an investment or savings.

I could feel them laugh at me as I left but I was determined though, no matter how small the amount, I was going to start somewhere. I finally found a building society that would allow me to put my contribution into a fixed deposit at a reasonable interest rate. Naturally, the more I put in the better, but I committed to a small unit trust and I paid in to that every month diligently.

Shortly after that I decided to put a very tiny amount of money into three fixed deposit accounts, one for each of my children towards their future education needs and one for us as a savings toward a deposit on a house or towards large items of furniture that we may need. It really was a very small amount of money that I scrounged from the grocery budget and little bits from each area of our budget, but for the first time in ten years, I started to feel like I was getting somewhere. It seemed to lift a huge weight off of me. It's hard to explain, but these financial commitments didn't carry the same 'burden' that the debt used to carry.

This seemed to make the load that I had to carry much lighter. I was actually working towards something in our monthly budget for the first time, even though our financial situation was probably the worst it had ever been. Once I had tasted the 'freedom' of investment, I started to realise that we also need to invest in the Kingdom of God.

If investing in the world's system were such a positive experience, how much more positive would it be to invest in a stable and uncorrupted system like God's one? We have always been people who tithed and we have always tried to give generously, knowing that God would give us returns and take care of us. I had never quite seen this as an investment opportunity. I began to make small allowances in our budget for "Kingdom investments".

Small amounts of money that we would give to the needy or as God would lead. Like any other investment, you need to be patient and wait for the returns, but they do come. And this is a sure investment; God's economy is not shaken and unstable like ours. It's the surest investment that you could make.

As we went through this terrible process of living by faith until we found the answers, I realised a few things. First of all, note the "living by faith until we found the answers" section. Am I living by faith because I need to until I find an income? It's terribly hard to live by faith, so it's not my preferred method of income. I began to try and see it as a lifestyle that maybe God would call us to live.

If so, the end goal shouldn't be a steady income, but the end goal should be to have peace while living by faith. Secondly, I found these hard times terribly draining and de-motivating. I would wake up some mornings, go to the bathroom and cry uncontrollably. I couldn't tell you what about, it was just the heaviness of the load I was carrying and the path that I walked and it was so hard.

As I walked this path, willingly I might add, I began to realise that my best times were when I was studying the word of God, or just talking to him. I found incredible strength in Him. As long as I was focusing on Him I found a great strength and was able to see opportunities that He would bring my way. The following is a story of someone I knew who was in a similar situation to us, and God provided in so many ways. This is what they had to say:

"We have learnt SO MUCH through these times and God has been faithful. He showed me a distant relative in the UK that I should write to with regards to my daughter's fees for further study. I have never met this man in my life but have communicated over the years with him on and off. He is 72. Anyway after I had written to him and posted the letter I just wanted to get it back from the post box – my thoughts were WHAT WOULD MY MOM SAY IF

SHE KNEW WHAT I HAD DONE? I didn't care if he said no, but I could picture him writing to my Mom and saying what a cheek your daughter has got and that was what I was more worried about! To cut a long story short he has given us £4000! The Lord just blows me away with His generosity and I think the lesson I have learnt the most is you have to put your pride in your pocket and humble yourself most of the time when you are in this place of need - He rarely drops anonymous envelopes off in your post box (He has done that at times) but more often than not you have to ask for help – He shows you who to ask.   The people He has led me to ask have always been so generous in their giving and haven't made me feel 'small' or embarrassed.

"I want to be what I was when I wanted to
be what I am now."

-   Graffiti, London 1980

Enjoying Each Moment

I read this quote and chuckled, maybe I am at the beginning of this quote and who says I won't feel like this person later on. I realised that I shouldn't despise the day of small beginning but embrace all that is happening in my life as an exciting journey. We will never know our future and we will never know where we will end up. Life is so unpredictable and there are no guarantees. It is really important that we enjoy each moment of our life because what we see as a struggle now may be a fond memory some day. No matter how hard it was, because we will see a fuller picture and we may even see the reason why it happened.

I am finding more and more that we should just trust God and rest in Him. If you have not applied the principles in this book or if you know that you have been disobedient, then you will not find that rest. It's best to put things right with God first. But if you know that you have done what God has asked, you need to rest and trust because He is faithful and His promises are 'yes and amen'.

During a season of severe lack, I felt that God was asking me to wait. Sometimes God asks us to do things that we don't understand and don't know why. Our friends may give us a hard time about it and we may sway between doing what God says and doing what they say. In the worst possible time of my life I had chosen not to find a job but to wait and in the waiting I chose to write what I believed God would have me write. I spent six month staying at home writing from nine to five, choosing not to work despite the lack of income at that time.

At the end of the day, He is the only one who can ever know what's in the deepest parts of your heart. Your secret desires and the true you. He alone will provide for you - your complete being - and he alone will do it perfectly. The rest is only an Ishmael - us helping Him along.

I wondered what He meant. He quite simply said "wait". "Don't go looking for a job, don't go looking for a ministry, just go about your daily routine, spend time with me and wait." If God has ever said that to you, you know how hard it is. 'Doing' is far easier than 'being'. I felt guilty about being so relaxed and I felt guilty about not bringing any money in, especially since there was no income at all at the time. I had pressure from friends that said I was silly (not in so many words though.)

I had family that were very unsupportive of my conviction and a whole lot of other pressures. The testimony that I want to share with you is probably the most powerful thing that I have ever experienced. In my waiting I have found an inner peace that I have never had before. I have learned to trust God completely by choice. Too often we have faith because it is the only option that we have. Lord, I don't have food so I am going to trust you for food. That's great and it's faith, but it's either that or take out a loan.

It's not your first choice. After ten years of walking in faith, I **chose** faith for the first time. God said wait and I waited. I waited while we had no income and I waited when income came. In that time I had come to understand that what God wanted from me was a choice, not just faith due to circumstances but a lifestyle of faith forever no matter what. Once I had made that decision I was set free. I had begun to experience real peace.

Another wonderful thing happened in that time. I was able to get to the place of making long-term plans by going from the thirty-day payday-to-payday cycle. That is very easy when there is no payday! I moved into an eternal cycle. I know that sounds really silly, but that's the way I see it. For the first time in my life I was able to rest in God's eternal providence and start to sow into His eternal plan.

It was no longer a case of looking out for finance to cover the month's bills and I was no longer giving my tithe simply because I always have out of habit or because I knew I just had to! Now I was able to give when God said give, tithe out of joy and look for opportunities to bring an offering to him.

Hilarious Giving

To give our last penny instead of going shopping was a joy. He provided extravagantly and we gave hilariously. All in all a joyous picture wouldn't you say? Now I can truly say that I am excited when it comes to tithing time, it's a genuine joy that's unexplainable and supernatural.

I continued to wait and see what God had in store, I didn't make any excuses to my friends and family because, I had seen and tasted that the Lord is good and once you taste that you don't want to eat anything else.

During the season of waiting and writing, I wondered how I would finish my testimony before I publish this book. I considered that perhaps publishing the book and the income from it would be the testimony, so I continued writing without knowing what the end of the story would be.

A few days after I had finished writing the first draft of this book, God dramatically changed our circumstances where we had substantial income and a rent free. I am living proof that God can and will provide. It is entirely possible that the testimony is not that God has made me rich financially, but possibly that I can be content in all things as Paul says in Philippians 4:11-13 "I am not saying this because I am in need, for I have learned to be content whatever the circumstances. I know what it is to be in need, and I know what it is to have plenty. I have learned the secret of being content in every situation, whether well fed or hungry, whether living in plenty or in want. I do everything through him who gives me strength."

Once God had turned our circumstances around, I found life to be a whole different ball game. I always imagined that once we had "plenty" the pressures would lift. I was very wrong, now the pressure was even more. I had enough money to care of all my needs and a whole lot of wants, now I have to use this money wisely. It seems that with added income God expects added responsibility from our side. The ball was in our court now and if we were wise and obedient with what God has given us He can give us more but if we fail in our responsibility He could take it all away again.

That sounds very harsh and God does not threaten us in any way, but there is truth in that. We have to be responsible because God wants us to have more. I believe that God is looking for wise people who can manage finances and be of use to Him in His Kingdom.

I found that it was easy to stray from all that I believed in and easy to be tempted in the wrong direction. After having needed so much for so long it was easy to justify buying and spending. After struggling for so long it was easy to say that we "deserve" a break! The pressure had not lifted but became more because now there were temptations all around us that never applied to us previously. Previously it was never a temptation to buy things on credit because I knew that I wouldn't qualify for a loan.

Now that finance was more plentiful and stable there was suddenly a whole new world to explore, new options to consider that were never options before.

My income was multiplied by six, for the first time EVER I was not poor. I had enough, more than enough. This also meant that now was the time to be wiser than before, more responsible and more determined to live a life pleasing to God. When your income is increased, so is your tithe and offering. Suddenly I was giving away an awful lot of money away, in fact I realised that my tithe was almost the same as my previous salary. The important thing was still to be as faithful with my giving as I was before when I had little.

If you do find that you have gone to the next level, the level where you do have money, beware of spiralling out of control. It is easy to spiral out of control very quickly and end up in debt. I found that because you can suddenly afford 'it' you think that it is easier for you to pay back moneys owed in a month or two. You can find yourself in a worse position before because of debt, and then you are right where the devil wants you.

Try to start out by giving more than usual, keep yourself focused on the Lord and see what He wants you to do with your money. After all He did give it to you for a purpose, not just for the sake of being rich.

"And God is able to make all grace abound toward you, that you, always having all sufficiency in all things, have an abundance for every good work."

-   **2 Corinthians 9:8**

Paul is careful to emphasise throughout that the only basis for this exchange is God's grace. It can never be earned. It can only be received by faith. Very often our 'abundance' will be like that of Jesus while He was on earth. We shall not carry large amounts of cash, or have large deposits in a bank.

But from day to day we shall have enough for our own needs, and something over for the needs of others.

Poverty No Longer Rules

One important reason for this level of provision is indicated by the words of Jesus quoted in Acts 20:35 'It is more blessed to give that to receive.' God's purpose is that all His children should be able to enjoy the greater blessing. He provides us, therefore, with enough to cover our own needs and also to give to others. This aspect of the exchange may be summed up: He became poor with our poverty that we might become rich with His riches.

Poverty no longer ruled my life; money was no longer a problem. Plenty was the order of the day and it was wonderful. Life changed dramatically and finally I was living the life I had always dreamed of. My children had what they needed when they needed it; we had a large home and a new car. Food was plenty and even luxuries were a part of our life. After so many years of extreme poverty it felt like I was rich. Of course I wasn't really rich but by comparison to the years of struggle I had experienced, my current circumstances definitely felt rich. Yet, for some reason, my heart was not satisfied.

I shopped to try and fill the void but there was still a void. I studied to get better educated but still the void remained. I started drinking more wine, because now I could afford it, but the void remained. Something was still missing. All these years, I thought that if I could just get some financial security, then I would feel better inside. Sadly this was not true. Nothing changed inside of me. I was still unsatisfied with life and still craved more. Even though I had more money I continued to find ways to get even more. Life was good, life was better but inside had not changed one bit. In fact I may have been worse off because I no longer depended on God as I did in the past. My heart was further away from God than ever before. Money had started becoming more important to me than God. I had tasted the good life and wanted more.

It wasn't long before Mo and I had returned to A as usual, lost our source of income yet again and found ourselves in exactly the same position as always. I reasoned that we needed to change A dramatically, so we moved from South Africa to England hoping to find a more stable life. In terms of finances life was much better. We had more security than we had ever had before but this still did not satisfy. After only a few months in England we separated and shortly after that got divorced.

God's blessings did not amount to anything in my life, not because God was not providing but because I did not know how to be a wise steward of what He had given me.

It was in my time as a single mum, in a place of total dependence on God, that I finally learned the lesson of stewardship. During all those years of lack and all those times of plenty, I never actually learned much about stewardship. No matter how many miracles God did in my finances or no matter how many ways He found to provide for me, I had never learned God's ways.

Basically God bailed me out every time I got in a pickle. During my years of being a single mum He continued to bail me out but He also impressed upon me the importance of stewardship. All my life, in the area of finances, God provided just like He promised He would[13], but it was like He was throwing money into a piggy bank that had no cork in the bottom. God's blessings did not amount to anything in my life, not because God was not providing but because I did not know how to be a wise steward of what He had given me.

No matter how little or how much money you have, whether you are living hand to mouth or are a wealthy banker with a six figure income, you can be guaranteed that your money is not safe if you do not understand the Godly principles of stewardship. If you are not doing things God's way you will eventually lose everything. Luke 16:1-13 contains everything we need to know about wise stewardship.

The Parable of the Shrewd Manager

Jesus said to His disciples: "There was a certain rich man who had a steward, and an accusation was brought to him that **this man was wasting his goods**. So he called him and said to him, 'What is this I hear about you? Give an account of your stewardship, for you can no longer be steward.'

Then the steward said within himself, 'What shall I do? For my master is taking the stewardship away from me. I cannot dig; I am ashamed to beg. I have resolved what to do, that when I am put out of the stewardship, they may receive me into their houses.'

So he called every one of his master's debtors to him, and said to the first, 'How much do you owe my master?' And he said, 'A hundred measures of oil.' So he said to him, 'Take your bill, and sit down quickly and write fifty.' Then he said to another, 'And how much do you owe?' So he said, 'A hundred measures of wheat.' And he said to him, 'Take your bill, and write eighty.'

So **the master commended the unjust steward** because he had dealt shrewdly. For the sons of this world are more shrewd in their generation than the sons of light.

And I say to you, **make friends for yourselves by unrighteous mammon**, that when you fail, they may receive you into an everlasting home. He who is **faithful in what is least is faithful also in much**; and he who is unjust in what is least is unjust also in much. Therefore if you have not been faithful in the unrighteous mammon, who will commit to your trust the true riches?

And **if you have not been faithful in what is another man's**, who will give you what is your own? "**No servant can serve two masters**; for either he will hate the one and love the other, or else he will be loyal to the one and despise the other. You cannot serve God and mammon.

Stewardship Principles from Luke 16

1. This man was wasting his goods (v1)

"Give an account of your stewardship, for you can no longer be steward," was what the master said.

This is also what Jesus says to us, "Tell me what you are doing with what material possession and money I have given you and if you are wasting it I will take it away from you."

Our material possessions and finances are given to us to better serve God not to take our heart away from God. Are you using every possible thing that you have in your possession to serve God? Is your home a warm and inviting home where people are welcomed and can find the love of God? Or is it picture perfect but cold and kept for your personal enjoyment?

Do you use your car to help get people who don't have a car to church or are you concerned that they damage it or use up your precious petrol? How about the food in your kitchen, are you getting fat because you eat too much or thin because you are obsessed with losing weight or are you really not concerned with either but use your food to feed others. Is your food eaten around a table with other people who don't know Jesus or do you and your family eat in front of the TV and focus little on each other and other people?

I could go on and on, analysing each of your household items and the money in your bank account, but I am sure you get the picture. Do you often pray for people at church to find solutions to their problems but seldom share your money? The Bible is clear on this, and says that if *one of you says to them, "Depart in peace, be warmed and filled," but you do not give them the things which are needed for the body, what does it profit?*[14]

Perhaps you are enjoying your life right now and are not bothered about what I have said. Be warned, your season of plenty might not last forever and when you are in need you will reap what you have sown. Make sure you are investing your money in the right places – the stock market can crash at any time, all it takes is one more natural disaster or terrorist attack. Heavens economy is secure, invest your treasure there and your heart will follow[15]. If you are not sure where your heart is, read your cheque book or your bank statement. What you spend your money on is a sure indicator of where your heart is.

2. Master commended the unjust steward (v8)

...because he had dealt shrewdly. It wasn't that God commends fraud or dodgy dealings. The commendation here was *because he had dealt shrewdly.* He had very quickly summed up the situation, taken control and sorted out a solution. Shrewd can be defined as having sharp powers of judgment or having a keen awareness. Resourcefulness, especially in practical matters, sharpness, intelligence and an intuitive grasp of practical considerations, can also define shrewd. Prudence, discernment, and farsightedness are other words commonly associated with shrewd.

These are the qualities that Jesus commended and that He also said that the sons of light often lack. As Christians we are sons of light! This is worrying that a dodgy dealer actually had better instincts than an honest Christian. We need to learn from this parable and ask God to teach us to be shrewd so that we can maximise our financial gain.

3. Make friends for yourselves by unrighteous mammon. (v9)

This is not a suggestion that you can buy your way into heaven but the truth is that one's stewardship is a test of one's relationship with God. Money can be your friend if you understand that it is a useful tool and not a master. Friend in this verse comes from the Greek word *'philos'* which means an associate, neighbour – it quite literally means friend. If you continue to read that verse it says so *that when you fail, they may receive you into an everlasting home.* A curious verse don't you think? Basically it is saying that you should develop a healthy relationship with money so that when you die you will go to heaven.

As you may well know, the Bible also says *it is easier for a camel to go through the eye of a needle than for a rich man to enter the kingdom of God*[16]. Why is this? My guess is that because very few rich men have a healthy relationship with money – they are unable to let it go if they need to, to the point of not being able to enter heaven.

I have heard many stories of wealthy men being challenged to give all their money away to the poor into order to pursue a humble ministry. Some have responded well and their story is amazing, how God many times restored the wealth they gave away to even more than they had before and gave them a flourishing ministry. Others, sadly, could not give up their wealth and ended up with nothing. Few rich men can have a healthy friendship with money, in order to find a healthy friendship with money they will need to give up all their money and start to live a life of trusting God.

Few rich men can have a healthy friendship with money, in order to find a healthy friendship with money they will need to give up all their money and start to live a life of trusting God.

He will give to them the amount of money that they can cope with, an amount that will not cost them their place in heaven. It's a scary thought that some people can put a price on their eternity.

4. He who is faithful in what is least is faithful also in much (v10)

God tests our level of stewardship on unimportant, earthly things. Once He is satisfied that we can manage well then He will entrust us with Kingdom things – *true riches*. Only once you have truly handled true riches can you really appreciate how insignificant money and possessions are. Ask God to allow you the privilege of a mission's trip or a ministry experience, something that requires your faithfulness in true riches. You will be changed forever and the value you place on mammon (assets) will be changed forever too. If you are faithful with the little opportunity He gives you, He will open the doors for more.

If you have a little bit of money or material possessions, start using it for Kingdom purposes and not for your own selfish gain and see how quickly what you have starts to grow. In our church recently we saw this principle in action so clearly. A couple were struggling financially, he has recently lost his job and she worked part time for very little money. They had been seeking God for their purpose in life and were very frustrated with how their life had turned out. His biggest frustration was the lack of money in his life. He was fed up with the hand life had dealt him and wanted more of everything.

After a few months, they slowly started getting involved in church life. They began to care for people and invite people over for dinner at their home. At one point they realised how their previously picture perfect home was suffering wear and tear from their visitors. Although this upset them they quickly resolved that this was simply a part of the price they had to pay in order to be used by God and His purpose in their life.

Their world was totally rocked when one day a congregation member, someone who had noticed their struggle and that their oven was broken, bought them a brand new convection microwave. Suddenly it all made sense, they had sacrificed their ideals and the value on their mammon but God has given them what they needed. They were faithful with the little that they had and God was beginning to give them more.

I have friends that have lived by this principle for many years, one friend gave away a car and reaped a better car, another friend had lived her entire life for God and was given a house – yes given a fully paid up furnished house. It might start with a microwave but I know that this family will be faithful with their microwave and cook many meals for people; I can't wait to see what God adds next.

5. If you have not been faithful in what is another man's (v12)

... *who will give you what is your own?* It might be easy to be wise with the little that God has given you, but what about what someone else has trusted you with? How do you manage your employer's time and money? This is a whole other ball game, why should you fret about how you use someone else's mammon? Well, the Bible says that if you don't you will not get your own? Starting small, you could consider how you treat a person's home that you are visiting or the way you treat your church. Do you clean up after yourself, do you show respect to the furniture or buildings? This is the very beginning of being faithful with what is another man's. In this day and age the challenge to be faithful at work is a big one.

Do you waste your employer's time by spending hours on Facebook or surfing the internet? Do you steal stationary, food if you work at a restaurant or your employer's time? God is watching all these things, and He measures your attitude towards your employer to decide if He can trust you with His riches.

My eldest daughter, Lorah-Kelly, is a brilliant example of this. She has served faithfully at our church for years, often using her own limited resources from her part time job to care for people. She is a great daughter too and has added value to our family by being faithful with what we have. Lorah-Kelly seems to attract blessings like I have never seen before. She has more than most people her age but she has not sought it or acquired it by her own efforts. For some reason as she gives of everything she has she seems to receive everything she needs!

6.   No servant can serve two masters (v13)

You will *be loyal to the one and despise the other. You cannot serve God and mammon.*   Mammon and God are opposite sides of the coin, they are black vs. white, darkness and light. There is no way that is it possible to serve both simultaneously. Right now at this point in your life you are definitely serving one or the other – I am one hundred percent sure of this.   God or material things – which one is more important to you? You will happily sacrifice the one in order to gain the other.   Which of the two are you most willing to give up?

I can assure you that you can't lose when you give up mammon but giving up God could result in losing more than you could ever imagine. Sadly, I have seen too many people take the blessing that

God has given them and turn it into an idol, into their master. The most common example I have seen of this taking place is when someone in our church is unemployed. During their struggle with unemployment and financial needs, they grow closer to God as they depend on Him and seek Him for a solution. God is wonderful and in every situation I have seen Him provide employment, some even self-employment.

Many, in fact all of those people were faced with a choice. I cannot think of one of them who did not face this choice. Which master would they serve? The master that provided the employment or the mammon that resulted from the employment. The choice ALWAYS comes when the blessing comes. Every person is tempted with money at some point in their life; we cannot escape facing this temptation. Once we face it and make a definite decision we will be able to determine who our master will be.

If we could grasp this concept then life would be much easier. Here are some choices that people have to make?

1. Do I work on Sundays?

This is the most common decision that I have watched people face. Ninety percent of the people that I have observed truly believe that working on Sundays is harmless. Of those people that express that belief not one of them have stayed in church!

Julian was unemployed due to mental health issues. For years he had been unable to work and lived a comfortable life on benefits. When he first started coming to our church we noticed that he was not happy with his life even though all his needs were met through government financial support for the mentally ill. Something was still missing, perhaps meaning or purpose. As time passed he became stronger as a person and so we began to pray for a job for him.

An opportunity arose for him to go into the same work he had done before suffering with his illness. He was delighted and immediately got stuck into his job. When he received his first pay cheque he was so happy that he couldn't wait unit Sunday to tithe, so he visited us at home and asked if he could give his tithe then and there. Eric and I were over the moon with joy to see the freedom that Julian had come into both in health and in finances.

Each month his church involvement got less as work demanded more hours from and within six months from his first day at work he had stopped tithing completely and had disappeared from church life. When bumping into him recently it was noted that he seemed desperately unhappy and mentally unstable again. The blessing that God gave him turned into his god. He stopped serving God and begun serving mammon.

The blessing that God gave him turned into his god!

Others have followed the same pattern. Teenagers getting their first job are so thrilled with their new found financial freedom that they ditch church to make more money. It isn't long before their lives are showing the fruit of their new god. Men with financial goals become obsessed with overtime to reach their goal and it isn't long before their new god takes their heart away from God and church.   Ditching church for work is a bad move, I have never, EVER seen any good come out of it.

2.   Do I stop giving to save?

If you understand the principle of sowing and reaping then you will understand how ludicrous this question is. Just consider a farmer asking the same question? Should he put his seed in the barn and see how long it lasts him or should he continue sowing it so that he can reap a harvest in due season? Yes, definitely keep a portion of your harvest for saving but don't keep the entire harvest as savings or you will run out in no time.

Why do most people find it easier to be generous when they have little but difficult when they have more? Think about it and whether or not this applies to your life too?

Practical Stewardship

If you really want to become a wise steward and would like some practical suggestions in financial management then I recommend that you get a copy of the Money Matters Workbook. This is a practical book that gets down to the nitty gritty of financial management, debt, saving, investing, budgeting, etc. I have kept a clear record of everything that I did during my season as a single mother that led me to financial freedom.

What God did in that season was so incredible. God met me more than half way as I committed to sorting out my finances. He gave me keys, ideas for being shrewd and even performed miracles to help me get out of debt and get on my feet. Most single mums will tell you that their standard of living drops significantly when they have to make it on their own but I can honestly say that my life went from strength to strength in every possible way. His provision was perfect, His mercy was great and the things He taught me about money and stewardship have changed my life forever.

To get down to some practical money management and for loads of money saving tips, get yourself a copy of the Money Matters Workbook.

For more information please go to
www.moneymattersbook.co.uk

Chapter 8

Renewing Your Mind

Renewing Your Mind

Proving God's Will

"For you know that grace of our Lord Jesus Christ, that though He was rich, yet for your sakes He became poor, that you through His poverty might become rich."

- **2 Corinthians 8:9**

When did Jesus become poor? Some people picture Him as poor throughout His earthly ministry, but this is not accurate. We can assume Jesus did not personally carry a lot of cash, but at no time did He lack anything He needed either. When He sent His disciples out on their own they had everything they needed too[17]. Jesus and His disciples made a regular practice of giving to the poor, this too is not something a poor person would do[18].

Jesus' methods of obtaining money were at times unconventional, but money has the same value, whether withdrawn from a bank or the mouth of a fish[19].

Jesus lived as we should in that He always had all that He needed to do the will of God, which we can have too if we trust in God's providence. Jesus was also continually giving to others, which again is something we should always be doing. Surely there is a connection between His supply never running out and His continual giving?

If this is the case then when did Jesus become poor for our sakes? The answer is simple: on the cross. Moses gave us the keys to understanding true poverty in Deuteronomy 28:48 where he highlights four things that define poverty: hunger, thirst, nakedness and need of all things. Jesus experienced all these elements on the cross. This is when Jesus became poor for us.

Consider these four things and then consider that you don't need to suffer any of them. Jesus took what should have been our suffering upon Himself, so that we never had to suffer again.

He was *hungry*.

He had not eaten for nearly 24 hours.

He was *thirsty*.

One of His last utterances was "I thirst!"[1]

He was *naked*.

The soldiers had taken all His clothes from Him[2].

He was *in need of all things*.

He no longer owned anything whatsoever.

In Corinthians 9:8 Paul presents more fully the positive side of the exchange: "And God is able to make all grace abound toward you, that you, always having all sufficiency in all things, have abundance for every good work."

Reading this book will achieve absolutely nothing if you don't receive all that Jesus has done on the cross. He has a made a way for us to be financially free. The journey towards financial freedom begins at the cross and from there it's a journey of applying Godly financial principles to your life. The Bible has provided us with ample guidelines and resources with regards to finances.

---

[1] John 19:28
[2] John 19:23

The following verse makes it very clear that we should transform our minds, and the best way to do that is to soak yourself in the Word of God daily.

"Do not conform any longer to the pattern of this world, but be transformed by the renewing of your mind. Then you will be able to test and approve what God's will is – His good, pleasing and perfect will."

-   **Romans 12:2**

Most of the financial patterns that we have adopted are not God's ways. Unfortunately, this has led many of us astray and put us in debt or in bad spending habits. In order to truly find financial freedom you need to change how you think about money. For this purpose I have created a thirty day reading plan that will assist you with renewing your mind in the area of finances.

My desire is that you would read the devotions one day at a time and meditate on each verse. There are spaces provided for your own notes at the end of each days reading, jot down ideas as they come to mind. Allow God to speak to you personally concerning your finances, and allow the Word of God to renew your mind completely.

There are approximately 2080 verses pertaining to money in the Bible, this must mean that this is an important subject to God. He wants us to have success in this area. I have taken thirty of the verses and put them into a daily devotion format to aid you in the renewing of your mind.

The most important thing to keep in mind is that Jesus has made a way for us to have success and victory in all areas of our lives. He died our death that we might share His life, and this relates to every single area of our lives, including the area of finances.

If you are serious about renewing your mind in the area of money please get a copy of the Money Matters Devotional. For more information please go to www.moneymattersbook.co.uk

Most importantly, if you truly want to serve God and not mammon, you need to start at the very beginning, at the place where you can put your life right with God. If you have never accepted Jesus

Christ as your Lord and Saviour then you will not understand why I speak so passionately about having only one God. *People who aren't spiritual can't receive these truths from God's Spirit. It all sounds foolish to them and they can't understand it, for only those who are spiritual can understand what the Spirit means[20].*

I tell you the truth, unless you are born again, you cannot see the Kingdom of God[21]. Being born again is simply allowing God to bring your spirit to life and you can do this right now by praying a very simple prayer asking Jesus to come into your life, by declaring that you will serve God and by allowing the Holy Spirit to begin an awesome, life changing work in you. It's incredible what God has planned for you and once you let go of your way and embrace His way, your life will be dramatically changed in every single area, including finances.

If you are ready to take this step, please pray the guide prayer that follows. Feel free to say what you have in your heart to say to God. There is no right or wrong way to pray, it is simply a chat with God.

Living Life Series – Money Matters

Dear Lord Jesus,

Today I want put my life right with you. I want to be free from all this fear and lack of peace. I want to give myself to you 100%. I say yes to your offer of perfect love and I gratefully receive this love now. I thank you that your death on the cross made it possible for me to be clean and to be free.

Please wash me clean today so I can have a brand new start. Please forgive me of all my past sins. Please fill me with your Holy Spirit. You are my Lord and Saviour now.

Amen

If you have prayed this prayer I would love to hear from you. Please get in touch at

angela@d7church.co.uk

About Angela

Angela is the mother of four, pastor of D7 Church, author and song writer. Born in Crawley, she spent all of her childhood in South Africa and now lives in Cheltenham with her Brazilian husband, Eric.

Angela has a passion to see people reach their full potential. In particular, she has a heart to see women set free from the lies that the enemy has fed them. She has published many books which covers the issues keeping today's women from being free.

She also writes a Blog about being a 21st century princess www.kingsdaughters21.co.uk and hosts an outstanding UK women's conference www.kingsdaughtersconference.co.uk

Other Books *by* Angela

Hope's Journey

"There was a time when all I wanted was to die but now that I have tasted life I really don't want to die until I have truly lived!" Hope's Journey is a heart wrenching account of Angela's struggle with depression & suicide.

Hope's Journey STUDY GUIDE

We all need HOPE. Hope's Journey STUDY GUIDE is about working together to find the hope that we have lost - a practical study to help you find a healthier mental, emotional and physical life for self-study or group studies.

Secure on the Rock

Every little girl wants to know that their daddy thinks they are beautiful! As we grow older that doesn't change we still longs to hear the words, "You are beautiful". But what if your daddy didn't call you beautiful but hurt you and did things he shouldn't?

Secure on the Rock STUDY GUIDE

We have all been through "stuff" that has robbed us of our security - it's time to take back what is rightfully ours. Secure on the Rock STUDY GUIDE is about finding security together ideal for self-study or small group studies.

Passion & Purity

"God made us girls for extravagant, wild, imaginative, adventurous, fantastic loving!" Angela openly shares of how her search for passion ended up in adultery and how she managed to find a way back to purity.

Passion & Purity STUDY GUIDE

Is your marriage lacking 'spark'? Are you good friends but not passionate lovers? Get that spark back and live as God intended you to live - with extravagant, wild, imaginative, adventurous, fantastic loving!

Being a Woman

"What is the true meaning of being a woman?" The heart of a woman screams to be free to love extravagantly and to live intentionally. A refreshing read with lively discussion from six women - it's NOT at all what you might think.

Being a Wife

Being a Wife is a follow on from Being a Woman where we go into the Biblical role of the wife in depth. A refreshing read on being a wife with lively, real discussion with a group of every day ordinary women - it's NOT at all what you might think

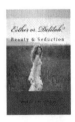

Esther or Delilah

An honest look at how women use their beauty to seduce men! Whether you like it or not you are using your beauty for something, but are you using it to empower a man or are you using it in a way that leaves him powerless? Esther or Delilah. Which woman are you?

He Restores My Soul

Do you ever feel like you are stuck on a treadmill that is set too fast and you cannot find the stop button? Modern living can often feel just like that at times. Stress, heart attacks, family breakdown and so much more is the result of the way we live our life these days. Press the pause button, take a deep breath, and uncover a much better way to live your life.

Free

Living life the way it was meant to be. There has to be more to life than this! What am I here for? What is my purpose? Who am I really? I have to find myself! Am I good enough? Who am I? "*Free*" explores all these nagging questions.

Nature's Way

You have the right to know that the government doesn't review the safety of products before they're sold. You have the right to practical solutions to protect yourself and your family from everyday exposures to the chemicals that modern health and beauty products contain. Exercise your rights today and begin taking care of yourself NATURE'S WAY.

The Tale of a Church Planter

The ups, downs, frustrations, joys and everything in-between on the roller coaster ride of church planting. I can honestly say that no recipe or formula for church building exists - God does not work in this way! D7 Church is proof of this. Not because we didn't try, we did try just about everything.

It was only when we gave up and said so to God that we began to have breakthrough. This is our story.

Money Matters

Are you tired of trying to get through each month, living only to make ends meet? Have you read all the books that promise 'seven steps to financial freedom' but lead you nowhere? Or are you someone who has plenty of money but can't find any satisfaction in life?

Money Matters has powerful, yet easy to understand principles that will radically revolutionise your view of money.

Money Matters
Simple Truths Leading to Financial Freedom

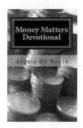

Money Matters Devotional
Renewing the Mind in the Area of Finances

Money Matters Workbook
Sort Out Your Money One Step at a Time

References

[1] John 8:32
[2] SKY TV Guide December 2001
[3] Hosea 4:6
[4] Proverbs 23:12
[5] Philippians 4:19
[6] Genesis 3:21
[7] Mark 12:17
[8] Matthew 6:24
[9] The Spirit Filled Life Study Bible *Footnote*
[10] Psalm 35:27
[11] James 1:2
[12] John 10:10
[13] Philippians 4:19
[14] James 2:16
[15] Luke 12:34
[16] Matthew 19:24
[17] Luke 22:35
[18] John 12:4-8; 13:29
[19] Matthew 17:27
[20] 1 Corinthians 2:14 (NLT)
[21] John 3:3: (NLT)

11868210R00132

Made in the USA
Charleston, SC
26 March 2012